FAMILY AND KINSHIP IN
EAST LONDON

Michael Young is Director of the Institute of Community Studies, President of the Consumer's Association and of the National Extension College and Chairman of both the International Extension College and the Open College of the Arts. He has also been President of Birkbeck College, University of London, since 1989. His publications include *The Rise of the Meritocracy* (Pelican 1961), *Innovation and Research in Education* (1965), *The Elmhirsts of Dartington* (1982), and *The Metronomic Society: Natural Rhythms and Human Timetables* (1988).

Peter Willmott is a Senior Fellow at the Policy Studies Institute. Chairman of the Institute of Community Studies and Visiting Professor of Social Policy and Administration at the London School of Economics. His other books include *The Evolution of a Community* (a study of Dagenham), *Adolescent Boys of East London* (Pelican 1969), *Community in Social Policy* (1984) and *Social Networks, Informal Care and Public Policy* (1986).

The authors were founder members of the Institute of Community Studies and have also written jointly *Family and Class in a London Suburb* (1960) and *The Symmetrical Family* (Penguin 1975).

FAMILY AND KINSHIP
IN EAST LONDON

*

MICHAEL YOUNG
AND PETER WILLMOTT

Foreword by Judith Stacey

UNIVERSITY OF CALIFORNIA PRESS
Berkeley · Los Angeles

University of California Press
Berkeley and Los Angeles, California

First California Paperback Printing 1992

Library of Congress Cataloging-in-Publication Data

Young, Michael Dunlop, 1915-
Family and kinship in East London / Michael Young and Peter Willmott.
p.   cm.
Originally published: London, England ; New York, N.Y., USA :
Penguin Books, 1986.
Includes bibliographical references and index.
ISBN 0-520-07897-7
1. Family—England—London. 2. Kinship—England—London. 3. East End
(London, England) I. Willmott, Peter, 1923-   . II. Title.
HQ616.15.L66Y68 1992
306.85′09421′2—dc20   91-35769
                                                                      CIP

Printed in the United States of America
9 8 7 6 5 4 3 2 1

The paper used in this publication meets the minimum requirements of
American National Standard for Information Sciences—Permanence of Paper
for Printed Library Materials, ANSI Z39.48-1984. ∞

TO DOROTHY AND LEONARD

FOREWORD

It cheers me to celebrate the reissue of a U.S. paperback edition of one of my favorite books. When the caprices of commercial publishing decisions forced me to drop *Family and Kinship in East London* from the required reading slot it had long occupied in my family sociology course, I initiated a modest one-woman lobbying campaign for a University of California Press paperback edition. It was gratifying, but unsurprising, that this proposal elicited unanimous, enthusiastic support from a diverse array of scholarly consultants surveyed—anthropologists, historians, architects, urban planners and sociologists. For this best-selling classic of British sociology is truly a book for many scenes and seasons.

Perhaps *Family and Kinship in East London* is best known as a landmark study of the social consequences of urban renewal policies in post-war England. The provocative challenge the book presented in 1957 to prevailing urban planning and housing policies, which ignored and thwarted the human relationships of the low-income populace who were their intended beneficiaries, earned it immediate and lasting attention. Yet it is oddly fitting, and a measure of the book's enduring, yet versatile, merits, that a feminist family sociologist and aficionado of ethnography, rather than an urban planner, should now instigate its American revival. For *Family and Kinship in East London* is at once a model of the serendipitous delights of the ethnographic method and a treasure trove of pregnant case material for diverse analytical and instructional purposes.

In their Introduction to the 1986 edition, Michael Young and Peter Willmott modestly acknowledge the twin features of their book that I most appreciate: "As happens so often with research, more interesting than what we were seeking was what we stumbled on—a highly articulated network of kinship relations." The authors had set out in 1953 to assist the British Labour Party by studying the effects of its housing policies on a working-class district in the historic East End of London. By the authors' own lights, however, the urban policies and political fortunes of the Labour Party failed to reap tangible benefits from their study's exposé of the social costs of relocating working-class East Enders to high-rise New Towns outside the metropolis. The political costs to the Labour Party and to British society I leave for others to assess. Yet, as a book, *Family and Kinship in East London* must be judged a phenomenal success. Perhaps the most widely read book of British sociology in the U.S., it is one of the first, and still one of the best, ethnographic studies of working-class family ties in industrial society.

The richly articulated working-class kinship relationships that Young and Willmott "stumbled on" and documented in vivid, engaging prose posed a challenge as well to the prevailing wisdom of fifties-era family sociology in the United States. Dominated by Talcott Parsons's theories of the functional fit between the modern isolated nuclear family and industrial society, most family sociologists of the period consigned the extended family to the nostalgic dustbins of preindustrial society. Clearly few had ventured very far into the communities of urban workers. For when Young and Willmott did so, even a small child of one of the authors was able to offer an ethnographic contribution to undermine this thesis. Returning one day from an East End school, he reported: "The teacher asked us to draw pictures of our family. I did one of you and Mummy and Mickey and me, but isn't it funny, the others were putting in their Nannas and aunties and uncles and all sorts of people like that."

Looking backwards after more than three decades of family scholarship generated by the no longer "new" social history and by feminism, such a discrepancy in definitions of family between social classes and between theory and practice is no longer so surprising. Scores of studies and critiques have discredited once-dominant views about how modernity homogenizes and contracts family ties. This makes it difficult to fully appreciate the novelty and insight of Young and Willmott's early contribution to these projects. *Family and Kinship in East London* is neither a historical study nor an overtly feminist one. It was conceived, conducted, and interpreted by men more than a decade before the resurgence of Western feminism and the rethinking of family theory the movement inspired. Yet its ethnographic method and findings are crucial to the efforts of feminists and social historians to de-naturalize "the family" by specifying and historicizing the diversity of gender and kin arrangements people continually construct beneath and despite this monolithic ideological shield.

Scrupulous ethnographers, Young and Willmott transcended the limitations of their gender as well as those of the modern nuclear family ideology of their period in their discovery of a rich, extended kin structure centered around and activated by women. When they astutely identified the extended family as "the women's trade union, the source of informal mutual aid for women and children, and for men too where they were in need of support," Young and Willmott were the first to plant an analytic seed feminists would sow and harvest for decades to come. Here *Family and Kinship in East London* can be seen as an inspirational forerunner to Carole Stack's analysis of African-American women as central kin strategists and survivalists in *All Our Kin*, to studies of women's "kinship work" in diverse ethnic communities such as Patricia Zavella's *Women's Work & Chicano Families* and Micaela di Leonardo's *Varieties of Ethnic Experience*, and quite directly to *Brave New Families*, my own ethnographic study of white, working-class, "postmodern," extended families in California's Silicon Valley.

Moreover, by studying the effects of urban relocation policies on working-class families, Young and Willmott managed to capture ethnographically one of the social sources of what in the United States has proven to be an ephemeral stage of male-breadwinner, nuclear family life. As the twentieth century approaches its terminus, this once-normative family structure has come to appear an aberration. Rising proportions of single-parent and "nonfamily" households fuel contemporary, alarmist accounts that family ties have been fatally wounded by new villains such as postmodernity, feminism and "secular humanism." Yet ethnographic research of the sort Young and Willmott inspired continues to reveal the resilience and creativity of women's extended-family, "trade union" strategies. While the family ties of the rising ranks of unemployed and underemployed male victims of postindustrial occupational dislocations do seem distressingly fragile, women continue to bear disproportionate responsibilities for maintaining children and other kin. Many have been renovating their historic "trade union" to cope with postindustrial challenges by forging complex new forms of extended family life, even those which incorporate relatives acquired via remarriage. Many women still find the extended family to be their most reliable form of social insurance.

And now another generation of American students enrolled in courses in sociology, anthropology, urban planning, community studies and many other fields will be able to find in *Family and Kinship in East London* the insight, knowledge and plain pleasure it has so reliably provided for others. If the "ethnographic present" it describes serves now as a historical document of family and social change, and if the book's realist and unreflexive mode of representation strikes some postmodern readers as somewhat innocent and quaint, *Family and Kinship in East London* still serves too as evidence of the fruitfulness of the ethnographic method for a multitude of disciplines, and as an inspirational model of engaged and engaging scholarship.

Judith Stacey
November 1991

CONTENTS

LIST OF TABLES

NEW INTRODUCTION

In 1890 Engels described East London as 'the largest working-class district in the world'. During his century London expanded from a city of one million people to more than four million, and within it East London was a city inside a city. With boundaries almost as strongly marked as those of some countries it was a city of the poor. To be poor, especially to be poor *en masse*, was at that time to be part of the low life which it was the duty of high-minded and high-collared people to reform. East London used to be 'darkest London', dark at night for lack of light, dark by day for lack of muscular middle-class Christianity. It would have been a surprise if Dickens had put Fagin anywhere other than Bethnal Green Road or Morrison chosen anywhere else for his hero than the Jago.

The citizens of East London were there partly because they waited upon the well-off who lived up-wind, to the West. The poor made clothes and furniture for the rich and some of them penetrated the class barrier physically by walking there or, when buses and trains arrived, by riding there to serve the comfortable classes, just as nowadays the blacks from Soweto travel into Johannesburg or from hundreds of other shanty towns journey into the centres of their metropolises. After dusk East Londoners returned to the little houses where they and their larger families lived just as now they return to the tower blocks which have largely replaced their former houses on the ground.

That was one reason we chose Bethnal Green as the site for the Institute of Community Studies, and for our first study. We needed a working-class district with bad housing, which was in those days a signal for renewal. We had both worked previously in the Research Department of the British Labour Party in the most formative period of the

xiii

welfare state, between 1945 and 1951. Pleased as we were by what had been done in general, we were less so by what we saw as a gap – and a widening one – between the Labour Government and its supporters. We wanted social-ist policy to be alive with the interests, hopes and fears of the people whom the policy was supposed to benefit, and, in our enthusiasm, we saw research as one of the keys. Social research was rare in Britain then, inside or outside the universities. We thought we could use it to find out about the needs of electors, of working-class families in particular, and publish the findings in books which would not have too much jargon in them. Housing policy, and particularly its impact in a working-class district like Bethnal Green, was an obvious subject to choose.

As happens so often with research, more interesting than what we were seeking was what we stumbled on – a highly articulated network of kinship relations. This proved to be relevant to housing policy and to many other matters besides. The existence of so many extended families meant that we could enlarge the scope of our inquiry. We could go wider than housing and embark on one of the first post-war ethnographic studies of a working-class district.

Once we had decided to follow our nose instead of our plans we were able to go some way towards uncovering the way of life of a settled community held together by informal relationships. A new welfare state was being consolidated while we were walking the local streets and knocking on the local doors. Behind that formality stood the rudiments of a much older organization, the kinship-based structure which has preceded the State as a method of government not only in Bethnal Green but in most of the world. At the time the survey was done, the extended family was, as we put it, the woman's trade union, the source of informal mutual aid for women and children, and for men too where they were in need of support. With so many relatives living locally there was less pressure and less of a weight of expectation for married couples to bear on their own. Children were still growing up with grandparents on the spot, being almost as much part of their family life as their own parents.

The working classes have always suffered from forms of denigration idiosyncratic to each period of history. But there have been certain common themes. Manual workers are said to be shiftless, lazy, improvident, rascally, uncultured, acting for themselves alone. We could not, on the basis of what we found, subscribe to any such condemnation. On the contrary the people we saw over a period of years seemed to us to have developed a way of life which could in some respects be regarded as a model for those who were (and still are) doing the denigrating. Poor, Bethnal Greeners may have been, especially the families with many young children, the old, the widowed and the handicapped. But if they were, their poverty was accompanied by a sense of family, community and class solidarity, by a generosity towards others like themselves, by a wide range of attachments, by pride in themselves, their community and their country and by an overflowing vitality. This was at the time a rather new view of people in the bottom reaches of the class structure which has remained so marked and consistent a feature of British society throughout the century; it was a view which may have influenced to some extent the manner in which such people were regarded rather more widely.

In the last thirty years a great deal has happened to the locality, apart from the housing which we will come to in a moment. It is, above all, clear that Bethnal Green has become part of an 'inner city area', with all that implies for the new kinds of deprivation suffered by such areas in London and the other cities of the Western world.

This is most evident as a result of the arrival of a new wave of newcomers. New immigrants to London have usually stayed close to their point of arrival. The Irish who have augmented the city's population have not settled in the East End. This is because they travelled the last leg of their journey by train, not boat. Many of the later ones stayed near the two stations where they arrived, Euston (for Camden Town and Islington) and Paddington (for the district immediately around the station, as well as Willesden). The West Indians had a different destination, Waterloo at the end of the line from Southampton, and formed a series of settlements in South London, with a particular clustering in Brixton; or came to Euston from Liverpool and from Euston to Islington and Hackney. The Indians and Pakistanis who came by air had their terminus at Heathrow and many of them settled nearby, in Southall and neighbouring districts.

The newcomers to our part of London are from Bangladesh. As far as London is concerned, they belong to an older tradition. East London was 'the largest working-class district in the world' because it abutted on the largest port of the world, with all its attendant trades and industries. Through that port have come wave after wave of newcomers who have each in turn enriched the life of the East End, London and the nation. The Huguenots entered that way and stayed nearby, in and around Spitalfields, which at their insistence became a centre of the country's textile and clothing industry. Then, in the nineteenth century and into the early years of this, Jewish immigrants from Russia and Eastern Europe arrived by the same route, fleeing from religious persecution, and landing in the docks as the Huguenots had done before them.

As parts of Bethnal Green could a century ago have been mistaken for Eastern Europe, so now could Brick Lane at the western end of the old Borough sometimes be mistaken for a city in the Indian sub-continent. Again it is largely because the area used to be so near to the port. Ships were still coming there in the 1950s when our study was being made. Merchant seamen from Sylhet and other parts of Bangladesh left their ships and found cheap housing in the district and jobs in the clothing and other trades, and brought their families over later. As so often happens with immigration (and as we discovered among the people we followed out of Bethnal Green to their new homes in Essex)

xvi

the first few were the pathfinders who marked out the territory for those to follow.

Beatrice Potter (Webb after she married) wrote about this very same district in 1888, in a chapter she contributed to Charles Booth's *Life and Labour of the People in London*[1]. This was at the height of the Jewish immigration. She said:

In this quarter thirty or forty thousand Jews of all nationalities and from all countries congregate, and form in the midst of our cosmopolitan metropolis a compact Jewish community. Judisch is a language of the streets, and Hebrew characters are common in shop windows and over doorways. Overcrowding in all its forms, whether in the close packing of human beings within four walls, or in the filling up of every available building space with dwellings and workshops is the distinguishing mark of the district.

And so it is today. All a modern Potter would have to do to that passage is to substitute **Bangladeshi** for Jewish. It is happening again, with the same rank prejudice against newcomers, the same exotic shops and signs and dress, the same brimming vitality, the same grinding poverty and the same extended families as the principal means of mutual support. Some of the newcomers are even employed in a few of the Jewish clothing workshops which have managed to hang on from the previous migration.

Figures produced by the authorities tell something about this new, and perhaps final, chapter in the old story. In 1951 less than one in 200 of Bethnal Green's population had been born in the Commonwealth. By 1981 the proportion was one in nine, and still rising. The Inner London Education Authority has also produced some comparisons. Owing to the influx from Bangladesh, Tower Hamlets (incorporating Bethnal Green) shows up worse by a good way than any other educational division of London. The proportion of Bangladeshi children with both parents unemployed is about 50 per cent. The estimated proportion of primary school pupils in Tower Hamlets eligible for free

1. Vol. 4, pp. 37–8. Fuller details about books and articles cited can be found in the *List of References* at the end of the book.

school meals is well over 60 per cent and the estimated proportion of pupils in Tower Hamlets who do not speak English at home is nearly 50 per cent.[1]

There are two reasons why it may never happen again. First, immigration to this country has been almost completely halted by successive Immigration Acts. Secondly, the port has gone. Reduction in foreign trade, containerization, transfer to other ports, the growth of road and air traffic have almost killed the Port of London, except down-river at Tilbury. After one of the immense time-lags for which Britain has earned a reputation some adaptation has taken place. The river used to turn its back on the city. Its stance is beginning to be reversed. The first hotel for a century has been built at St Katharine's Dock. The Isle of Dogs is on the way to becoming a new town and industrial estate across the river from Greenwich. The East End is undergoing another transformation in its economic structure. If the economy of Britain recovered from its present deep recession there might even be a return to (or towards) the full employment which Bethnal Green enjoyed when we were pattering down the streets with our sheaves of papers and our eager plans.

*

The particular reason for being in Bethnal Green was, as we have said, that our first inquiry was to be about the effects of rehousing policies on working-class family and community life. The district for study had to be one in London which had a predominantly working-class population and from which people had been rehoused in large numbers. Bethnal Green was right on both counts.

Our initial idea was simply to interview people in Bethnal Green and in 'Greenleigh', a suburban housing project to which people from Bethnal Green had moved, to

1. *Educational Priority Index: Changes Between 1983 and 1985*, Inner London Education Authority.

see how their lives had changed. This remains one of the main themes of the book.

It is obvious that, because of the importance of the system of kinship – which became the core of our study – the effects of the official policy on the family were even greater than we had imagined. When young families were rehoused away from Bethnal Green they were cut off from their relatives, and from the mutual aid thus provided. Contrary to the stereotype, they had not been socially isolated where they lived in the city. But they certainly were after the move, particularly in contrast to what they had been accustomed to.

Our study was of people moved by the authorities to new municipal suburbs, and some explanation of the administrative arrangements is needed for a modern reader. Britain has a long tradition of municipal housing. For nearly a century local authorities sought to deal with the problems of poor housing by building and managing a stock of their own, first inside their boundaries and later outside as well. The London County Council (LCC) derived its powers to do this from the Housing of the Working Classes Act of 1890, which concentrated on the need for action in London. The 'Boundary Street' estate, built in Bethnal Green in 1895, was the first large-scale housing project in England. (We did some of our interviews there in the 1950s and it was still standing, refurbished, in 1985.) Boundary Street was the first of many in London and in every other town and city in Britain. The pace of municipal building increased between the two World Wars, and even more after 1945.

In the 1950s, there were two municipal authorities for the district of our study – the local council, the Metropolitan Borough of Bethnal Green, and the LCC, covering what was then 'London'. In 1966 the structure changed. The London County Council gave way to the Greater London Council, extending over an area more than twice the size, and the local boroughs were amalgamated to form larger units with greater powers within Greater London.

(The latest change, in 1986, abolished the GLC, leaving the boroughs with still greater powers.) In 1966 the Metropolitan Borough of Bethnal Green was, for instance, merged with the Boroughs of Stepney and Poplar into the new London Borough of Tower Hamlets. At the time of our study both tiers of London government had housing powers. The Borough Council built within its own boundaries. The LCC built not only throughout all of London, but also outside it, on virgin land that it was able to buy for the purpose.

Despite the improvements due to earlier municipal effort, after 1945 housing remained worse in the East End than elsewhere in London. Most people lived in small houses, rather than flats, but the houses had often been badly built and badly maintained, and many were still occupied by more than one family. So the London County Council gave particular emphasis to building new homes for East Enders, and many of these were outside London.

In the post-war period the main objectives of planning and housing policy were two-fold, in London as in the other British cities: to improve conditions in the older districts and to halt the unplanned spread of suburbs into the countryside. Inside London, both the London County Council and the Borough Council demolished slums, replacing them with blocks of flats rather than houses, on the reasoning that this would provide spacious homes and open space without creating more urban congestion. Outside London, the LCC complemented the Government's post-war programme of New Towns (of which eight were to be built around London) with large housing-estates, and Greenleigh was one of these.

The two councils rehoused families whose present homes were to be demolished as slums or who were judged as in acute 'housing need', for instance because of bad health or severe overcrowding. Families in slums due for demolition would be given new dwellings by the Borough Council or the LCC depending on which authority was demolishing their old home. A family rehoused from a slum by the

Borough Council would go to a flat in Bethnal Green; one rehoused by the LCC could choose a flat inside London (not necessarily in Bethnal Green) or a house on an estate outside London, like Greenleigh. Those families who thought that they deserved a new home because of their 'housing need' could register with either authority or both, but they stood a better chance with the LCC – as long as they agreed to move to an estate outside London.

This description of how people from Bethnal Green were moved to Greenleigh does not take account of the voluntary movement out from the East End that was going on at the same time. People who could afford to buy their home often chose to go to the private suburbs and sometimes beyond to country towns and villages. The process had started long before 1945. The population of the East End had been falling for half a century, most of the out-migrants being people who had wanted to go. With hindsight, we recognize that this point was largely neglected in our study. Even among those who left Bethnal Green after 1945 because of municipal planning, none was literally forced to leave. But, as we have explained, the official policy was to encourage movement out, and most of those we talked to in Greenleigh felt that they had to go if they wanted a better home.

The argument we put in the last chapter in this book still seems to us to be right. The policy issue is one of choice. If people wish to leave the city, and their relatives, that is fine. Nobody should want to stop them from going or force them to remain in close contact with relatives they dislike. But if they do not wish to move away from the established social network, and if public policy offers them no effective opportunity to remain, the unhappiness and the social costs are far greater than they need to be.

We would like to be able to say that these arguments persuaded politicians and officials. Our book was well-received. Extracts were published in the newspapers, the sales were a record for a report of a sociological study, government ministers quoted us. But the policies we advocated were not accepted until the late 1960s, and by then it was too late.

There is now a broad consensus in Britain that repudiates the post-war policies in London and the other cities. For twenty-five years government and municipal authorities were united in a gigantic folly. Criticisms like ours were bulldozed aside, together with the consistent evidence from opinion polls that most people disliked flats and high flats in particular.

It is not entirely clear why things went as wrong as they did. Part of the blame lies with the architects of the modern movement, and in particular Le Corbusier, whose vision of 'cities in the air' inspired two generations of British architects, including the architect-planners who were so influential in the key posts in central and local government in the period. Their desire to build up into the sky fitted in with a general reaction against the urban sprawl of the 1930s, and was endorsed by the structure of government subsidies. The initial assumption was that local authorities might be reluctant to build flats; later it was that they needed financial incentives to build high flats in particular. So urban councils first got, as well as extra help to buy expensive urban building land, a larger subsidy for flats than for houses and, after 1956, a larger subsidy the higher they built.

As Patrick Dunleavy pointed out in his analysis of the 'politics of mass housing' in the post-war period,[1] another important influence was industrialized building, using methods imported from the continent. Although the new 'systems' could be used for low-rise as well, the high-rise boom coincided with their increasing application in Britain. Looking back in 1973 to when he had been Minister of Housing, Sir Keith Joseph anguished, 'I suppose that I was genuinely convinced that I had a new answer. It was prefabrication and, Heaven help me, high blocks.' In general

1. Patrick Dunleavy, *The Politics of Mass Housing in Britain 1945–1975*, pp. 107–23.

the politicians of both Left and Right enthusiastically backed the architects and the big building firms. This was partly because of a desire – in response to public pressure – to build more homes, and build them quickly. It may also have been, as Peter Hall and his colleagues suggested in *The Containment of Urban England*,[1] that there was a 'sort of unspoken and unwritten compact between the Labour urban councils who wanted to maintain their rateable value and retain their working-class support, and the Conservative counties and their agricultural and rural allies who did not want council tenants spoiling their peace and threatening their electoral dominance'.

One of the most extraordinary aspects of this sorry affair is that in practice the new flatted estates had little in their favour. Though there were honourable exceptions, most of the blocks, high and low alike, were so barrack-like – so much the image of 'mass housing' – that they made the council's pre-war neo-Georgian blocks and cottage estates seem handsome by comparison. Because of the space needed around the building, little land was actually saved. In any case the fears of land shortage were unfounded. There were other sources – for instance, the unused railway marshalling yards that we mention in this book – and, since people were already flooding out of the cities, the pressures were less than was supposed, and less than we ourselves realized at the time. Furthermore, as Dunleavy showed, flats cost about half as much again as two-storey houses, and they consistently took longer to complete for occupation, partly because the first family could not move in until the whole block was ready.

Whatever the explanation for the collective madness, it certainly destroyed the neighbourhoods of small streets of houses in the older working-class areas and encouraged the movement out which was the subject of our research. In the process it replaced an urban environment at the human scale by a monolithic and impersonal one, breaking up

1. Peter Hall *et al.*, *The Containment of Urban England*, Vol. 2, p. 398.

communities of the kind we had uncovered in Bethnal Green. If the lessons had been learned in the 1950s, London and the other British cities might not have suffered the anomie and violence manifested in the urban riots of the 1980s.

The evidence of the 1981 Census, when compared with that of 1951, shows the scale of change. The population of Bethnal Green fell by about half, from 58,000 to 30,000. Much of the old housing was destroyed and replaced by municipal flats; the share of dwellings owned by the authorities increased from under a third to four-fifths. This policy led to improvements inside people's homes. Over the thirty years, the percentage of households living at more than one person per room fell from 20 per cent to 9 per cent, those without a bath or shower of their own from an incredible 79 per cent down to 5 per cent, and those having to share a wc from 37 per cent to only 1 per cent. But the process was damaging in two ways. First, the method of redevelopment: large areas were demolished and people had to move away not only from their old homes but also from their familiar area; many thousands of families went out of London in the way we describe in this book, others to different districts inside London. The second mistake, as we have said, was in the physical form of the new housing, which was out of step with the tradition of two-storey urban housing in Britain. The flats were almost universally detested by those who lived in them, and they created an environment in which it was difficult for social networks to be re-established.

As for the effect of these and other changes on community and kinship in Bethnal Green, we are of course unable to say what we would find if we repeated the survey now. One recent small-scale study in the area confirmed that the same kind of mother-centred kinship system still operated; the author reported that much of what we had said was 'replicated in the families involved in this study'.[1]

1. Jocelyn Cornwell, *Hard-Earned Lives*, p. 106.

So our findings would still hold at least for some people. But the importance is almost certain to be less. Anthea Holme's research in 1981 on the housing of young families, also done from the Institute of Community Studies, found that fewer people in Bethnal Green than in 1955 had relatives living near, that for most 'the mother-daughter bond had loosened' and that there was 'greater isolation from the surrounding community'.[1] This is consistent with the picture from recent studies we ourselves have done in two other London inner areas – Lambeth and Hackney.[2]

As for Greenleigh, Chapter 10 indicates our anxieties about the ways in which it might develop. We argued that it would be difficult for children, when they grew up and married, to live near their parents for two reasons. First, most of the migrants were growing families; when the children grew up and married there would not be enough houses for all those who wanted to stay, and there was no space to build more. Secondly, the then policies of the LCC reserved any homes that were vacant for new migrants from London. As with Bethnal Green, we have not done a further survey in Greenleigh to test our predictions, but some kind of assessment can be made.

One guide is a subsequent study that one of us carried out in Dagenham, an LCC estate built in the 1920s and 1930s.[3] The purpose of that research was precisely to answer a question posed by the present book: after forty years, would people still be isolated from relatives and neighbours or would kinship and community have been re-established? In brief, the answer was that, though Dagenham was in many ways unlike the Bethnal Green of 1955, at least substantial contacts with relatives, friends and neighbours had developed, and these were important in the daily lives of most residents. We believe that a study of Greenleigh now would show similar results. The problems

1. Anthea Holme, *Housing and Young Families in East London*, pp. 137–41.
2. Graeme Shankland, Peter Willmott and David Jordan, *Inner London: Policies for Dispersal and Balance*; Michael Young *et al.*, *Report from Hackney*.
3. Peter Willmott, *The Evolution of a Community*.

of the second generation, in particular, would have been further helped by the reorganization of London government in 1966. Because of that, Greenleigh now belongs not to London but to a new local authority, the Epping Forest District Council, which has therefore been able to offer vacant houses on the estate to some of the sons and daughters who wished to continue to live there after marriage.

Thus Greenleigh after thirty years has probably developed local networks fuller and more supportive than we believed possible when we made our original inquiry. In general, we were too gloomy about the future of such new places in the suburbs. But it would be wrong to imagine that Greenleigh is a reborn version of the Bethnal Green of the 1950s. The social patterns of the East End described in this book were particularly strong, supported by a traditional ethos and reinforced by the physical form of the densely-packed streets.

As we have said, when it was published *Family and Kinship in East London* portrayed a somewhat different picture from the conventional view then current of working-class life in older areas. It also cast fresh light on the housing and town-planning policies which were at that stage acclaimed by almost everybody except the people who were themselves affected. How do kinship, community and public policy appear to us thirty years later?

We have indicated that we would expect the ties of kinship and local community to be generally weaker than they were in places like Bethnal Green. This is of course not only because of the effect of the policies that we criticized, but also because of other changes – more voluntary movement out of the cities, the influx into them of people of different races and different ways of life, the general improvements inside people's homes and in communications over a distance, the increase in married women working and the feminist challenge to traditional roles.

These changes mean that kinship networks are more dispersed than they used to be. But there is plenty of evidence that kinship remains an important force in most people's lives, and is in particular still overwhelmingly the main source of informal care and support. The wider family shows an impressive resilience, adapting itself to change in the rest of society. At least, that is, as long as it is left alone. If official policies work against it, ignore its existence or fail to recognize its contribution as an instrument of welfare, society is weakened in consequence. The general argument of this book remains, in our view, as valid as when it was first written.

1986

INTRODUCTION

THIS book is about the effect of one of the newest upon one of the oldest of our social institutions. The new is the housing estate, hundreds of which have been built since the war. In the last century people moved into the cities; in this they have been moving steadily out again, towards the country-side from which their ancestors came. The middle classes led the exodus into the inner suburbs; the working classes of London and other large cities followed by jumping over the earlier settlers into the outer ring of municipal estates.

The old institution is the family. It has been official policy to move people out of the cities; and we felt it would help in the assessment of this policy if more were known about its effects upon family life. For our purpose, we needed to make a comparative study, in the place from which people had come as well as in the place to which they had gone. For the one, we chose a London borough, and for the other, an estate which was one of those built by the London County Council on the outskirts of the metropolis during the years after 1945. The book is divided into two parts; the first describes the borough and the second, the estate.

We were least prepared for what we found in the borough. The wider family of the past has, according to many socio-logists, shrunk in modern times to a smaller body. The ancient family consisted not only of parents and their child-ren but also of uncles and aunts, nephews and nieces, cousins and grandparents. Kindred were bound together through-out their lives in a comprehensive system of mutual rights and duties, which were almost as binding in the agricultural society of our own past as in some of the surviving primitive societies studied by anthropologists. But as a result of the social changes set in motion by the Industrial Revolution, relatives have, we are told, become separated from each other. In urban, if not in rural areas, children remain with their own parents only while they are still dependent. The literature of psychology, too, contains a great deal about parents, very little about grandparents.

We were surprised to discover that the wider family, far from having disappeared, was still very much alive in the middle of London. This finding seemed to us of more interest than anything we had been led to expect, all the more so when it transpired that the absence of relatives seemed to be as significant on the estate as their presence in the borough. We decided, although we hit on it more or less accidentally, to make our main subject the wider family.

This has so far been mainly the province of anthropologists. They have investigated kinship in more primitive societies where it is of so much greater importance than our own that the study of society is sometimes in large part the study of kinship. The vocabulary they have employed for describing such societies is not necessarily apt in describing our own. We have therefore felt it necessary to use certain special terms. When they marry, husbands and wives are already members (as we put it) of the 'families of origin' into which they were born. Three families are therefore involved in any marriage – the wife's family of origin, the husband's family of origin, and the new 'family of marriage' which they create. Each of the members of a husband's (or wife's) family of origin may connect him with yet other families – his (or her) parents with *their* families of origin, that is with grandparents and uncles and aunts; his (or her) siblings with *their* families of marriage and to the nephews and nieces contained within it.

Every relative is thus a link with yet another family, each family of marriage being knitted to each family of origin and each family of origin to each family of marriage by a member they have in common. The common member may be a mother who is also daughter and sister, a father who is also son and brother, a sister who is also wife and mother, or a brother who is also husband and father. The interlocking pattern is repeated in different forms throughout society in the way that is so familiar. We refer to all the relatives whom a person knows to exist, in all the families to which he is linked in this way, as his 'kinship network'.

*

The chosen borough was Bethnal Green in East London. Most of the 54,000 people it contained in 1955 belonged to the 'working class', in the sense that they were predominantly employed on manual work, in such locally important industries as furniture, clothing, transport, docks, and engineering. Contrary to a general impression, the great majority of the people were Gentiles; according to our survey, only about eight per cent of the population was Jewish. The chosen housing estate was 'Greenleigh'. We have given it a fictitious name in order to conceal the identities of our informants there who form a high proportion of ex-Bethnal Greeners on the estate.

We obviously could not see all the people in these districts. In fact we saw not many more than 1,000. But these were chosen rather carefully. We wanted, as far as we safely could, to talk about all the local people although we were seeing only some of them. This object was achieved by following the usual practice of sociologists and selecting 'samples' of people for interview. In Bethnal Green, for instance, we picked from the electoral register every thirty-sixth name appearing on it. We then called on each of the people whose name had come up in this way and asked if he or she would be willing to talk to us. Most of them were. These people were in what we call the *general sample*; in addition we interviewed a second or third time, and much more intensively, a smaller *marriage sample* of couples with young children. Further details about the samples are in the Appendix. We have, to conceal identities, given everyone a fictitious name.

Both of us worked either in the borough or on the estate throughout the three years in which the research was done. One of us also lived in the borough with his own 'family of marriage' for most of the time, and both his wife and his children, who attended local schools, provided further sidelights on the place. An example was the comment of the small son who came back one day from school to say, 'The teacher asked us to draw pictures of our family. I did one of you and Mummy and Mickey and me, but isn't it funny, the others were putting in their Nannas and aunties and uncles and all sorts of people like that.' As a result of this close connexion with the district, we came to know well a number of local residents who gave us full accounts of their family relationships which helped us to understand and assess the information given to us in the formal interviews. We also did what we could to check what people told us verbally by personal observation in homes, churches, clubs, schools, parks, public houses, and street markets. But we should say, what is as obvious as it is important, that for the most part we can only report what people say they do, which is not necessarily the same as what they actually do.

We should also make it clear that the research was done between 1953 and 1955. Our account is of the borough, the estate, and the London County Council's housing policy as they seemed to us at that time.

*

We would like to thank all those many people who helped us with this inquiry, and above all Dorothy and Leonard Elmhirst, Edward Shils, Richard Titmuss; our colleagues at the Institute of Community Studies – Philip Barbour, Daphne Chandler, Peter Marris, Peggie Shipway, Peter Townsend, and Phyllis Willmott; and Ann Cartwright and Margot Jefferys.

PART ONE

KINSHIP IN BETHNAL GREEN

I

HUSBANDS AND WIVES, PAST AND PRESENT

BETHNAL GREEN is part of a country which has been, within living memory, the scene of great social changes, and in this background chapter we shall notice their impact upon married couples. The rest of the book is devoted far more to the relationship between the couple and their families of origin than it is to husbands and wives. To describe the marital relationship in any detail would demand a different technique and interviews far more searching than the ones we were able to do. But husbands and wives are so much the principal actors of our study, through whose eyes we look at kinship, that we need to consider, even if only to register our impressions, some of the essential characteristics of their relationship.

When we started the inquiry we assumed that husbands and wives do enter into something much more than a formal relationship, of such significance to each of them that all their other family relationships have to be adjusted in consequence. This we might have continued to take as axiomatic had there not come to light some evidence to the contrary from previous investigations in working-class London. Poverty was, very understandably, the chief concern of Charles Booth and other research workers of the past. They chronicled the barefoot children in the streets, the undernourished babies in overcrowded tenements, and the young mothers dying for want of food and medical care, and laid the blame not only upon unemployment, low wages, and the high birth-rate, but also upon wrong spending, especially on the part of the husband. The husband too often took for himself what he should have spent on his family, an example, but a telling one, of his failure to cooperate with the person to whom God had joined him. One or two references will show

17

that we were well advised not to take our assumption for granted.

Our research has been done mainly in Bethnal Green. In 1896, Helen Bosanquet wrote of the neighbouring borough of Shoreditch:

> But who that knows the London poor does not also know the feebly apologetic smile with which the women will say 'Oh, I don't know what 'e *gets*; I only know what 'e gives me.'[1]

This was not the end of it. The husband was not only mean with money. He was callous in sex, as often as not forcing a trial of unwanted pregnancies upon his unwilling mate. He was harsh to his children. He was violent when drunk, which was often. According to a report on Lambeth, another of London's working-class boroughs, written forty years ago:

> ... the separation of interests soon begins to show itself. The husband goes to the same work – hard, long, and monotonous – but at least a change from the growing discomfort of the home. He gets accustomed to seeing his wife slave, and she gets accustomed to seeing him appear and disappear on his daily round of work ... Her economies interfere with his comfort, and are irksome to him; so he gets out of touch with her point of view. ... He makes his wife the same allowance, and expects the same amount of food. She has more mouths to fill, and grows impatient because he does not understand that, though their first baby did not seem to make much difference, a boy of three, plus a baby, makes the old problem into quite a new one.[2]

Being a prisoner to child-bearing, the wife could not easily mend her finances for herself by going out to work. She lived in the dread that even the little support her husband afforded her might be withdrawn by his unemployment, by his premature death, or by his desertion. Helen Bosanquet said 'as the children grow older the chances are that the

1. Bosanquet, H. *Rich and Poor*, p. 107. The findings of subsequent surveys about the housekeeping allowances given by husbands to wives are reviewed in Young, M. 'Distribution of Income within the Family'.

(Fuller details about books and articles cited can be found in the list of references at the end of this book.)

2. Reeves, M. S. *Round about a Pound a Week*, p. 155.

burden of maintaining the family falls entirely upon the mother. It is so easy now for the father to disappear and to take up life free of responsibility in some of the many shelters or lodging-houses in London.'[1] If these were the conditions of life, his wife did indeed belong to the downtrodden sex.

Even though we may think the accounts overdrawn, and distrust the representativeness of the families they describe, we cannot ignore the historical evidence, all the more so since the notion still survives[2] that the working-class man is a sort of absentee husband, sharing with his wife neither responsibility nor affection, partner only of the bed. Such a view is in the tradition of research into working-class family life. The one aspect of that family which has been amply described is its failure. Study has been piled upon study of all the things that have gone wrong, of juvenile delinquency and problem families, broken homes and divorce, child neglect and Teddy Boys, which together have created an impression that working-class families are disunited, unsocial, and unhappy. And in all this the villain is often the man. The woman is presented as struggling bravely on though worn out by her children, loaded with hardship and old before her time, sharing a house but not a life with a figure pictured as neither a loyal husband nor a dutiful father.

But it would be wrong to confuse past and present in the fantasy that life for manual workers, and their wives, is today the same as that which evoked such righteous horror from Mayhew, Booth, and Rowntree. There is no confusion in Bethnal Green. People are well aware of the change which has come upon them in the course of a few decades. Indeed it is because the comparisons they make between the old and the new are so much a part of their mentality, the source of much present exhilaration and perplexity, and because

1. Bosanquet, H. op. cit., p. 106.
2. See, for instance, Slater, E. and Woodside, M. *Patterns of Marriage*, which is also about working-class families in London. Dennis, N., Henriques, F., and Slaughter, C. *Coal is Our Life* similarly describes the men of a colliery village in Yorkshire.

the influence of the old is so clearly written upon the new, that the contrast properly belongs to an account of the impressions we have formed of present-day life. Let us consider a few of the main changes.

THE FALL IN BIRTH-RATE

The birth-rate, to take an example, has fallen in Bethnal Green no less than in the country as a whole. This emancipation of women has depended upon husbands even more than upon wives.

'Fifty years ago it was different,' said Mr Florence, one of our informants. 'They had more children than they could afford. The pubs were open all day, so far as I can understand. The man would spend all his money in the pub, come home, and abuse his wife. There was no birth control in those days, I know, but even then there were ways and means not to have children if you didn't want to have them. And if the woman complained, it was hold your noise and give her another baby, and that's the finish.'

Such an attitude still survives. When one husband said to us 'We wanted the baby,' his wife retorted, '*You* may have done; I know *I* didn't.' Asked later if she wanted more children, she said 'I don't want them, but you can't tell. You ought to ask him (pointing at her husband) about that. He's the guv'nor.' At another interview there was the following dialogue.

HUSBAND: The baby was my fault. I was to blame for her.
WIFE: Yes, you were drunk that night.
HUSBAND: Oh no, I wasn't. I *decided* we ought to have another.
WIFE: Go on, that wasn't how it was.

Another woman was persuaded by a local social worker to get herself fitted with a contraceptive cap. Two months later she turned up, pregnant once more. Asked what had happened, she said 'My husband wouldn't have it. He threw it in the fire.' The fatalism of the past is still reflected, too, in the expression a woman uses when she is pregnant. She says she has 'fallen'. 'We had been married eight

20

months before I fell.' 'Once when I found I'd fallen again I said I'd go somewhere about it, but I didn't bother.'

The point is not that the old behaviour survives but that it is now no longer dominant. Whatever happened in the past, the younger husband of today does not consider that the children belong exclusively to his wife's world, or that he can abandon them to her (and her mother) while he takes his comfort in the male atmosphere of the pub. He now shares responsibility for the number of children, as well as for their welfare after they are born. More common now is the husband who, like Mr Meadows, says 'We decided we wanted two and that's what we've got. We even planned their names, Kevin and Janice. We didn't start until after the war. Kevin (aged nine) would have been fourteen by now if it hadn't been for the war.' Or like Mr Merton – 'We don't want only two. I'd like three. So would she, but I say "Wait and see how we get on" – with the money, you know.' Or like Mr Banton – 'You can look after two – give them the best of everything. If you've got more, you can't do it. You always want to give your children better than what you had. People are more educated today; they know they can have better if they want to.'

In the past women, as one old lady put it, had 'one child always at the breast and another in the belly'. Now their child-bearing period is over much earlier, and more of them can, as a result, go out to work, when still quite young, in order to make their own contribution to the finances of the family. Many husbands acknowledge that when their wives also go out to work, they have a responsibility to do more to help in the home. 'If the wife goes out to work,' as one woman put it, 'then the husband's entitled to help'; and he usually does.

Or consider the effect of the falling death-rate. Table 1 shows the numbers of people born in different periods, whose homes were broken by the death, divorce, or separation of their parents while they were still children of dependent age, that is while they were still under fifteen years of age. There has been a fall in the number of broken homes,

TABLE I: Broken Homes in Bethnal Green
(General sample)

Year of birth	Number of people	Percentage of people born in each period whose homes were broken before they reached the age of fifteen, by:	
		Death of parent(s)	Divorce or separation
1890 or earlier	146	29%	2%
1891–1905	208	26%	1%
1906–20	273	17%	1%
1921–35	294	19%	1%
TOTAL	921	22%	1%

The number of people in this table is less than the total of 933 in the sample because information on this point was incomplete for twelve people. In some later tables, also, small numbers of people are excluded for the same reason.

almost entirely as a result of the drop in the death-rate, whose importance quite dwarfs the divorces and separations. And if we consider the experience of our informants in their own marriages (as distinct from their parents' marriages), then it is clear that in recent years there has been a further fall in the proportion of parents lost to their children. For this district we would confirm what Titmuss has said – 'It is highly probable that the proportion of broken marriages under the age of sixty, marriages broken by death, desertion, and divorce is, in total, smaller today than at any time this century.'[1] Disease is less deadly. Childbirth is less dangerous. The Second World War killed far fewer fathers than the first. As a result, both children and parents enjoy greater financial and emotional security than they did. The benefit to wives is obvious. When they marry and have children, they can look forward with more assurance than their mothers could to continuing support from their men.

1. Titmuss, R. M. The 'Position of Women', p.100.

22

FROM BAR TO HOME

Another big change is in housing. Many homes in Bethnal Green are still deplorable. In the old days they were even more overcrowded, uncomfortable, and dirty; more often than not shared with other families. Damp washing draped in front of the kitchen range, crying children, and a tired and disgruntled wife were all that awaited most men after a long and hard day's work. The men's refuge was the 'conversation, warmth, and merriment of the beer-shop, where they can take their ease among their "mates"'.[1] For many men the bar in the pub was as much a part of their living space as the room in their home, with the difference that one was more or less reserved for members of their own sex while the other was not. The 'rent' of a seat in the pub, measured in glasses of beer, was so much greater than that of a seat at home that the housekeeping allowance had to suffer. 'From the home point of view there was no enjoyment at all for the man,' said Mr Florence, 'so when he did get a bit of money he tended to go round the pub and spend it there.' Mr Aves remembered his own father:

'My Dad used to say, "I'm the man of the house. Here's my money. And if anyone wants me, you know where I am – in the pub."'

Since then standards have risen. For one thing, fewer families have to share houses. In 1931 there were, according to the Census, three households to every two dwellings; twenty years later there were five households to every four dwellings. New building and the higher earnings which have made it possible to afford higher rents have given more families a home to themselves. And, within the home, whether shared or not, living space is less cramped than it used to be. 'In the old days,' said one man with some exaggeration, 'they used to sleep ten in the bed and five up the chimney.' But in 1911 one out of every three people in Bethnal Green *did* live more than two to a room, and by

1. Mayhew, H. *London Labour and the London Poor*, Vol. I, p. 11.

1931 one out of every four were still doing so. By 1951 the proportion as overcrowded as this was only three in a 100. In twenty years, though the number of rooms in the borough was much the same, the population was halved by migration. Today's homes are less overcrowded and more comfortable. The pubs are still there in quantity, one to every hundred dwellings, and men still go to them more than women. The working men's licensed club does not admit women on Sunday mornings. 'It's bad enough letting them in here at all,' one man told us. 'Surely we can keep them out one day in the week.' But men do not go to pubs as often as they used to. All the publicans lament the loss of trade: the men stay at home with their wives and children. 'If they want a drink of beer now,' said one woman, 'they go and fetch a bottle in, so they can watch the tellie at the same time.'

Or consider the effect of the fall in working hours. At the end of the last century, as Booth discovered, the 'recognized hours' for french polishers were $55\frac{1}{2}$ a week, for market porters 72 a week, and for railway carmen 84 a week, to give as examples three occupations favoured then, as now, by Bethnal Greeners.[1] The reduction of working hours after 1918, and again after 1945, has made a difference to every family. The spread of the five-day week has created the 'week-end', a new term and a new experience for the working man. With it has come the new sight of young fathers wheeling prams up Bethnal Green Road on a Saturday morning, taking their little daughters for a row on the lake or playing with their sons on the putting green in front of the windows of the Institute of Community Studies.

'One good thing is that we have much shorter hours now than before the war. I'm all for the 5-day week – the 40-hour week. I remember my father used to work 72 hours one week and 60 the next. He was on shifts. The week he did the longer hours was in the day. We didn't see anything of him. I was in bed when he got back at night. People get more time with their families now.'

Fewer children, longer lives, more space in the home, less

1. See Booth, C. *Life and Labour of the People of London*, 2nd Series, Vol. 5, pp. 182–214.

arduous work – these are some of the changes which have profoundly influenced the local community. It has been penetrated at a hundred points by the great society. Ideas, as well as people, now move more freely. The popular press, the cinema, the radio, and now the television have put new models, drawn from other classes and other parts of the world, before the local people, creating new aspirations and new ideals. One illustration of the effect upon the family of the wider world is the practice about naming children. In the past, it was not uncommon for children, and especially sons, to be given the same Christian names as their parents, the eldest son often taking the father's and the eldest daughter the mother's name. In family after family, amongst the older people, the same names repeat – Mary, Alice, Ada, Elizabeth, Amy, Emma, Ivy, Margaret, Ellen, Jenny, Florence, Doris for girls; and John, George, Harold, Albert, William, James, Charles, Joseph, Henry, and Thomas for sons. One wife said that:

'My Mum thought it ought to be called Bill, after my husband, if it was a boy, and after me if it was a girl. With her its all family. She doesn't like all these fancy names.'

Despite such pressure, the practice has undoubtedly changed a great deal, as shown by Table 2.

The inheritance of names is clearly less favoured by the younger parents than it was in the past. Custom is being replaced by fashion, and the fashion does not spring from Bethnal Green. This is most marked with the boys born since the end of the war who now have names like Glenn, Gary, Stephen, Nicholas, Christopher, Graham, Adrian, and Kevin, and the girls such names as Maureen, Marilyn, Carol, Jacqueline, Janet, June, Susan, Gloria, Lana, and Linda, unknown to ancestors christened before the dawn of Hollywood.

THE EMERGING PARTNERSHIP

We do not want to overdo it – these changes have not worked a revolution. New couples, as we shall see, live close to

TABLE 2: Naming of First-Born Children

(General sample – 730 people with at least one child of own sex)

	Sons		Daughters	
Age of parent	Number of fathers	Percentage of fathers in each age group with first-born sons named after them	Number of mothers	Percentage of mothers in each age group with first-born daughter's named after them
20–29	30	20%	37	0%
30–39	103	21%	84	6%
40–49	78	41%	77	8%
50–59	65	60%	61	28%
60 & over	80	58%	115	38%

parents whose ideas were formed before the great depression. In a place characterized by continuity of family residence there cannot be a complete break with the customary outlook of the past. The old segregation of man and woman has not ended yet. It accounts for one of the defects of this book. In our earlier interviews we asked about husbands' earnings. But it soon became clear that many wives still do not know what their husbands' wages are. Helen Bosanquet would still recognize the apologetic smile. And if, in our search for reliable facts, we asked the husbands in the presence of their wives (in practice it is impossible in this kind of research to see all husbands alone, since when he is in, in the evening, so is she) for the figure of their earnings, some of them either mentioned a sum suspiciously round and general or became obviously embarrassed. Even when we asked wives, when themselves seen alone in the daytime, they were sometimes taken aback. 'Oh no, he wouldn't want me to say anything about his wages. That's his business.' The older men and women were less forthcoming than the younger. Since we did not want to create discord between our informants, nor prejudice our chance of the fullest cooperation during the rest of the interview by trying to get some material not vital for this particular inquiry, we decided that we could not properly continue to ask questions about earnings. This is why there is next to no material about them in our report. Our only finding is a negative one – we have no reason to believe that the ignorance mentioned so often by Rowntree and the other authors of the poverty surveys is markedly less than it was in the past.

Yet we cannot reconcile our other impressions with the stereotype of the working-class husband. The man's earnings may still be his affair, but when it comes to the spending of the money, his part of the wages as well as hers, husband and wife share the responsibility. 'To be truthful,' said Mrs Sanderson, one of those interviewed before we dropped the question, 'to be truthful, I don't know how much he earns, I only know what he gives me.' But she later went on to describe the discussion she and her husband had recently had about whether to buy a television set, which he would pay for, and to mention that 'My husband does a lot of the cooking; he's a good cook.' In the home there are still 'men's jobs' like cleaning windows, mending fuses, and decorating, and 'women's jobs' like cleaning, cooking, baby care, washing dishes and clothes, and ironing. There are still plenty of men who will not do 'women's work' and women who think 'it's not a man's place to do it.' But for most people, it seems, the division is no longer rigid. Of the 45 husbands, 32 gave some regular help to their wives with the housework; 29 had, to take an index trivial enough in itself but perhaps significant, done the washing up one or more times during the previous week. Booth does not mention men washing up.

IT'S ALL FOR THE KIDDIES

The sharing of responsibility is nowhere more obvious than over the children.

'There's certainly been a change. I whack mine now, but not the beatings like we used to have. When I was a boy most of us feared our fathers more than we liked them. I know I feared mine and I had plenty of reason to.'

'I had a very strict father although he drank. When I came home from school at dinner time he put me to work making the dolls. I had a long loose frock put over my other clothes to keep them clean so that the work would be hidden from the school. When I got back again at tea-time he started me on it all again until seven when I went to bed. On Saturday nights we had to crawl under the table to get out of his way.'

'Men like my father never did much around the house. He found it a strain to pour out a cup of tea. If he saw a man pushing a pram or carrying a kiddy, he'd say he was a cissy. It's all changed now.'

Nowadays the father as well as the mother takes a hand in the care of the children. 'It used to be thought very undignified for men to have anything to do with children. You'd never see a man wheeling a pram or holding a baby. Of course all that's changing now.' He no longer automatically gets the first pick of everything. 'Dad used to be very strict with us,' said Mrs Glass, 'we're different with our boy. We make more of a mate of him. When I was a kid Dad always had the best of everything. Now it's the children who get the best of it. If there's one pork chop left, the kiddy gets it.'

In 1938, as Titmuss has said, 'the London County Council's school nurses found that the clothing and footwear of elementary schoolchildren was 54.6 per cent good, 45.1 per cent fair, and 0.3 per cent poor. A study of the returns for individual metropolitan boroughs discloses a very low proportion of "good" ratings for certain areas, notably, Bethnal Green 7 per cent, Poplar 13 per cent, and Stepney 13 per cent.'[1] A similar survey today would tell a very different story, as the children's neat poplin shirts, unpatched trousers, crisp cotton dresses, and sturdy sandals testify. Not only do fathers, as well as mothers, have more money; they also take a pride in their children's turn-out.

Both of them now share in the hopes and plans for their children's future. More parents are keen, not just that their children shall get a job, but get a better job, and school, no longer a somewhat regrettable whim of the State, is increasingly seen as a means to this end. Parents who want

1. Titmuss, R. M. *Problems of Social Policy*, p. 117.

their children to enter white-collar occupations know that a grammar school is the essential qualification, and one which is no longer quite beyond their reach. Here are some of the things that fathers said to us about their sons – educational aspirations for daughters are as yet more rare.

'I'd like him to take up chemistry. It's completely unproductive and therefore well paid.'

'I want the boy to be a doctor or a farmer, not to work in a factory or be a porter like me.'

'I don't want him to be in manual work. I'd sooner he worked with his brains than his hands.'

Such ambitions, perhaps themselves the source of new strains and disappointments, are not, of course, held by everyone. A sizeable minority of men in Bethnal Green take a very different view from white-collar people about the status of manual work, placing jobs such as company director and chartered accountant towards the bottom of the scale and manual jobs, like agricultural labourer, coal miner, and bricklayer, towards the top.[1] These men regard business managers with disfavour because 'They're not doing anything. They get their money for walking around', and, as for civil servants – 'I could find other ways of using my money.' Agricultural labourers, on the other hand, they value highly because 'you can't do without grub'; coal-miners because 'without coal, industry stops'; and brick-layers because 'you've got to have food and after that you've got to have houses'. But even some of the men who take this view are anxious that their children should get as good a technical education as possible. We asked people in the marriage sample with children under eleven what sort of secondary school they wanted the eldest to go to and more than half of them wanted a grammar or technical school,

1. A special subsidiary inquiry was conducted into the prestige of different occupations, which has been reported in Young, M. and Willmott, P. 'Social Grading by Manual Workers'. The earlier study into the attitudes of a predominantly white-collar group was reported in Hall, J. and Jones, D.C. 'Social Grading of Occupations'.

anything other than what one woman called the 'ordinary'.

These preliminary impressions suggest that the old style of working-class family is fast disappearing. The husband portrayed by previous social investigation is no longer true to life. In place of the old comes a new kind of companionship between man and woman, reflecting the rise in status of the young wife and children which is one of the great transformations of our time. There is now a nearer approach to equality between the sexes and, though each has a peculiar role, its boundaries are no longer so rigidly defined nor is it performed without consultation. The grand assumption made by Church and State (but thrown into doubt by earlier surveys) can be re-established. Given that man and wife are partners we can now move on to the relationship of each of them with their two families of origin.

2

WHERE PEOPLE LIVE

WHEN they marry, though the man and wife of Bethnal
Green draw closer to each other, they do not break right
away from their existing relatives. Since they bring their
families of origin into their new lives as well as into the
church, they have to make a profound double adjustment:
to each other as individuals, and to the relatives who surround them. The wife has to reconcile her new obligations
to her husband with her old obligations to her parents, and
the husband likewise. The wife has to adjust to the husband's
family of origin, and he to hers. A marriage modifies all the
other family relationships of each of its partners no less here
than anywhere else.

Much depends on where the couple live. Their decision
helps to determine which of their relatives they see most; it
may also determine which family of origin they most closely
ally themselves with, the husband's or the wife's, and hence
the type of adaptation which has to be made by each of
them. In Bethnal Green few couples have much choice at
the start of their marriage. They have to find space under a
roof belonging to someone else, and, since there is little
enough of that, they have to put up with what they can
get.

So it is not surprising that many couples begin their
married life in the parental home. This was what twenty-one
of the forty-five couples in the Bethnal Green marriage
sample did immediately after their wedding. Of more significance for kinship relations is the fact that fifteen couples
lived with the wife's parents against only six with the husband's. From what people told us it was clear that this is
the preferred arrangement: if they have to share a house –
and particularly a gas stove – it should be with the wife's
parents. The reason is simply that mother and daughter are

31

already used to each other, while mother-in-law and daughter-in-law are strangers, and, what is worse, rivals for a stove and a sink – and maybe for a man.

In her own home the husband's mother is dominant. She has looked after her son all his life and knows (or thinks she knows) his little likes and dislikes far better than anyone else. Her daughter-in-law may seem an outsider trespassing in a province peculiarly her own; an outsider who threatens the mother's eminence in the household and her place in the affections of her son. The wife's plight may be worse. Coming with ideas about house-keeping formed by her own mother which may not agree at all with her mother-in-law's, she must adapt herself at one and the same time to the new relationship of marriage, a formidable enough task in itself, and to the ways of her mother-in-law. 'I didn't', said Mrs Banks, 'get on all that well with her when we were living with her. She starts cooking something and it's something you don't like, or she starts something in a way that you're not used to. It's different from the way that your own mother used to do it.' It is no wonder if she becomes as hostile to the mother-in-law as the mother-in-law is to her. Mrs Flood's experience is not unusual.

'I've got two rooms with my mother-in-law. I have to go down three flights for every drop of water, and as soon as I come into her kitchen, she turns her back. We never speak to each other even if we meet in the street.'

If the tension between wives and their mothers-in-law can be as sharp as this when they live together, why does anyone do it? The usual reason is that they have no choice. The wife's parents may simply have no room, and accommodation elsewhere be non-existent, so that the couple have to fall back on the husband's parents. However unwilling the wife may be – and of course she is not always at loggerheads with her mother-in-law – living with her is in the last resort preferable to not living with her husband. The wife can after all spend a good deal of the day with her mother.

'We lived at my mother-in-law's at first. She had the room and my mother didn't. Well, I say lived there – even when I slept round there I used to go round home during the day. I went on having my food round at Mum's same as before.'

In this way she may be able to make do until another place becomes available.

There is less chance of the wife being able to live with her parents if she is one of the first in the family to marry. The parents of the forty-five wives in the marriage sample had an average of 4.4 children alive. Their houses hardly ever contain more than two or three bedrooms, and are sometimes so small that, as one woman put it, 'when one breathes out the other has to breathe in.' The parents clearly have not got room, in houses of this kind, for four married children as well as for their husbands and wives. One married child is as a rule the most they can accommodate. Which one is it? Usually not the first to marry, for at that time the unmarried children are still at home. The first daughters married have either to go to the husband's parents (if he is an only child or one of the last to marry in his family) or wait until they can get a house of their own. Daughters who marry later have a higher chance of being able to live at home because their other siblings have already left it. Since the last daughter to marry is usually also the youngest daughter, one would therefore expect that more youngest daughters than others would be living at home. Only daughters are not, of course, handicapped in this way. They have no one to compete with them for space, and so, whenever they marry, can more easily live at home.

Some evidence can be obtained from the general sample. Table 3, which compares only daughters and youngest daughters with others, shows that more of them live with their parents.

Though it has many disadvantages, one compensation of living in the parental home after marriage is that, in time, at the death of the parents, the couple may acquire the tenancy for themselves. Their tenancy is the most valuable property-right many working-class people possess: where

TABLE 3: Married Daughters Living with Parents

(General sample – 388 married daughters of people interviewed)

	Only daughters	Youngest daughters	Other daughters
Living with parents	23%	16%	6%
Living elsewhere	77%	84%	94%
TOTAL %	100%	100%	100%
Number	71	80	237

the property is privately owned, the rent is low and controlled by law. Provided he is living with his surviving parent when he or she dies, a child can inherit it. Of the 633 people in the general sample who held the tenancy of their present house (or whose spouse held it) 44, or 7 per cent, had inherited it in this way, the inheritance being from the wife's parents about twice as often as from the husband's. Weekly tenancies may stay in the family for more than two generations. One woman told us her maternal grandmother had been first tenant of the sixty-four-year-old house in which she lived, her mother the second, and she herself the third.

Private landlords are in certain circumstances obliged by the Rent Restriction Acts to allow the surviving spouse or child living with the tenant to become the tenant in his turn. Public landlords are not under this same legal obligation, but, in practice, they usually behave in the same way, the London County Council and the Bethnal Green Borough Council acting like other local authorities. An inquiry was made into the transfer of tenancies of flats in the L.C.C.'s Boundary Street Estate. This is a vast cluster of tenement blocks, actually the first of the L.C.C.'s housing estates, built at the turn of the century. The records, which go back to 1908, show that, for the 955 dwellings, there have been 113 transfers upon the death of the sitting tenant. About half of these went to widows after their husband's death, and all but 11 of the remaining 58 to children. Of the 47 tenancies inherited by children, 33 went to daughters, 14 to sons.

Most of the couples who live with their parents do not want to, they have to. It is not just that there is so little space, becoming more and more crowded when children are born. It is not just that they have to share stove or water, bath (if any) or lavatory. If they have to share so much, the mother and father are also bound to get on the nerves of their daughter sometimes, and of their son-in-law more often. The proper thing in Bethnal Green is, therefore, to have a 'home of your own'; for most people anything else is a second best. Even when a couple is living with the parents and making no effort to get away, they still assert their belief in the ideal.

It is rather different where there is only one parent alive. By living with the widowed mother or father the children can look after them when they need care without having to divide their labours between one household and another. Relations are also apt to be smoother, because instead of there being two households under the one roof the widow or widower can easily join the one household, run for the most part by the younger woman. And there are not so many people in a restricted space. This was decisive for one couple we interviewed.

'It was through his Mum dying that we got married so early. I used to rush home to cook tea for his Dad. Charlie was already paying rent for his room so we said "Why shouldn't we get married?" I asked my Mum and Dad and they said "Yes", so I moved in there.'

But the couples who choose to live with parents are the exceptions. Most people do not want to live with them, they want to live near them. Mr Sykes, who lives near his mother-in-law said 'This is the kind of family where the sisters never want to leave their mother's side.' The Sykes family was not the only one, either inside or outside Bethnal Green, subscribing to this view. Another writer has reported that in Wolverhampton –

The fact that no less than four per cent of the sample had children living actually next door is astonishing; and there is no doubt that this proportion would have been higher but for the general housing difficulties since 1939, for the opinion was frequently expressed by both generations that this is the best mode of life for the old people, since it enables them to preserve their independence and the married children to live a separate life, while at the same time ensuring that help is at hand when needed.[1]

Dr Sheldon was writing primarily from the point of view of the old. That difference apart, his statement could stand as well for the people we have interviewed in Bethnal Green.

Very many people in fact succeed in achieving their goal. The whereabouts of the parents of married people is shown in Table 4.

TABLE 4: Proximity of Married Children to Parents

(General sample – 369 married people with at least one parent alive)

Parents' residence	Married men	Married women
Bethnal Green	50%	59%
Adjacent borough	18%	16%
Elsewhere	32%	25%
TOTAL %	100%	100%
Number	195	174

The difference in the proportions of men and women having parents living in Bethnal Green is small, so small in fact that it is not statistically significant. The important thing is that more than two out of every three people, whatever their sex, have their parents living within two or three miles – either in Bethnal Green or one of the adjoining boroughs of Hackney or Poplar, Stepney or Shoreditch.

If we consider only the parents living inside Bethnal Green, a marked difference emerges. The figures, given in Table 5, show that twice as many married women as men live in the same dwelling as their parents, and nearly twice as many in the same street or block. This suggests that resi-

1. Sheldon, J. K. *The Social Medicine of Old Age*, pp. 195–6.

TABLE 5: Proximity of Married Children to Parents within Bethnal Green

(General sample – 199 people with parent(s) living in Bethnal Green)

Parents' residence	Married men	Married women
Same house or flat	14%	28%
Same street or block of flats	14%	23%
Elsewhere in Bethnal Green	72%	49%
TOTAL %	100%	100%
Number	97	102

dence is (to use an anthropological term) more often 'matrilocal' than 'patrilocal', in as much as couples more often live near to the wife's parents than to the husband's. We can, as far as this district is concerned, corroborate Gorer's previous finding that there is 'a marked tendency towards matrilocality in the English working class'. 28 per cent of men in his national sample lived within five minutes walk of their wives' parents as compared with 19 per cent of women living within the same distance of the husbands' parents.[1]

ONE FAMILY'S STORY

An illustration may help the reader to visualize the houses we are talking about and appreciate the part played by the parents. Mr and Mrs Banton and their two young children live at present in a four-roomed house in Minton Street in the middle of the borough. The other houses (but not the two pubs, obviously newer) were all built in the 1870s, of brick which has become a uniform smoke-eaten grey. They are nearly all alike in plan; on the first floor two bedrooms; and on the ground floor a living room, a kitchen, and a small scullery opening on to a yard which has a lavatory at the end of it and a patch of earth down one side. Many of the

1. Gorer, G. *Exploring English Character*, pp. 45–6.

yards are packed with clothes hanging on the line, prams, sheds, boxes of geraniums and pansies, hutches for rabbits and guinea-pigs, lofts for pigeons, and pens for fowls. The only difference between the houses is the colour of the curtains and doorsteps which the wives redden or whiten when they wash down the pavement in front of their doors in the morning. Dilapidated but cosy, damp but friendly, in the eyes of most Bethnal Greeners these cottages *are* the place,[1] much more so than the huge blocks of tenement buildings standing guard, like dark fortresses, over the little houses. On the warm summer evening of the interview, children were playing hop-scotch or 'he' in the roadway while their parents, when not watching the television, were at their open windows. Some of the older people were sitting in upright chairs on the pavement, just in front of their doors, or in the passages leading through to the sculleries, chatting with each other and watching the children at play. Mr Banton was suspicious at first, but after a few minutes' talk on the doorstep, listened to intently by the neighbours, he let us in and called his wife. He was a small, downright man in shirt sleeves and braces; he looked (though he was not) much younger than his wife, who, at 35, was beginning to fill out into the figure of a Bethnal Green 'Mum'.

They told us that they were married in the last year of the war. She continued to live with her parents who had been given a house in Nantes Street when they were bombed out in 1941. When her husband was demobbed from the R.A.F. they took over the two small rooms at the top of the house. Though they were glad to have somewhere to live, they were not happy: they did all their cooking on two gas-rings and had to come downstairs into the parents' part of the house for water, sink, and w.c. They had to stay there for four years. Then Mrs Banton's widowed grandfather moved out of the house he had been occupying in the next street. Up

1. Since 1956, when this book was written, this has become less and less true. The Council's 'slum clearance' schemes have replaced many of the old streets of terraced houses with new blocks of flats and maisonettes.

to that time he had been looked after by an aunt who lived nearby, but when the Council pulled her house down, after declaring it a slum, and moved her to 'one of those estates outside London', she could not care for him any more. He went away into a Home, and thereupon the wife's mother spoke to the rent collector. He allowed them to take over the grandfather's tenancy, and there they still are. They are fairly contented, although Mrs Banton says 'I'm fed up with washing Dickie in the copper'; she would give a lot for a bath. She still goes around several times a day to see her mother and gets her shopping for her; her mother, although getting on in years and not so active as she was, is still able to look after her grandchildren whenever the need arises.

Other mothers help in the same way to get houses for their daughters. When one of them is going to get married, the mother makes it her business to get to know about all impending vacancies. Are the Harrisons really going to move from No. 10? Is old Mr Jones being taken away to hospital at last? She asks neighbours, she asks other relatives of hers, she asks her own rent collector and the others in the street, she asks the publican and the shopkeepers, she asks the estate agents. One of the largest estate agents in the borough confirmed what we had already been told in the homes – that it is nearly always the mothers who come to his office after houses for their daughters.

The mother is naturally more likely to know about people moving out, or planning to move out, in her own particular part of Bethnal Green. This is one reason why daughters get accommodation near her. Not only is her knowledge more complete, her influence with landlords and the rent collectors is also greater. She knows personally the man collecting her rent, who often does so for several other nearby houses, and very often it is he who in effect selects the tenants for any premises that become unoccupied. His main concern is to find one who will pay the rent regularly. He needs a personal recommendation. He gets it from the mother, or from some other relative, if he does not, indeed, already know the children well himself, and on this recommendation he acts.

Mrs Robbins, who lives in the same street with her mother and five married sisters, explained the process at its simplest.

'My mother has lived here for years and my sisters were all living here. We knew the collector and spoke to him. That's how we got this place.'

Of another street, Mr Trimble said 'Around here it's all a family affair – mother speaking for daughter and mother speaking for son and all that kind of thing.' Recommendation may not, however, be enough in itself. The agent may need a bribe as well, but if it is reasonable, the couple, or the parents, are usually prepared to pay.

'We got it through my mother's agent. We had to agree to do it up though and we had to give him a bit of dropsy.'

'Her Mum lived in Bethnal Green and she spoke to the landlord for us. She told him we'd pay ten quid if we could get in there.'

And one mother herself gave a bribe of £15 to get a vacant flat for her daughter.

Kinship counts, if anything, even more in blocks of tenement buildings than it does in the cottages. The explicit policy of some of the trusts is to give preference to relatives: one of them, the Nags Head Housing Society, has ruled 'that only children or other relatives should be entitled to vacancies'. The local superintendent of another justified the policy by saying: 'We prefer sons and daughters. They know all the rules through having lived here. They know what has to be done. You don't get no trouble with them.' But whether or not the official policy favours relatives, this is in practice what happens.

'If you're living in these buildings, it just goes on and on. If you've got any daughters getting married, they get a flat. Outsiders don't get it. It's all in the family.'

'All my family have lived round here. My grandmother came here as a child and brought up all her family here. My mother lived here before she died and my auntie lives here now. These places are all filled by tenants putting their names down for their children. They put them down on the waiting list when they get engaged. Then when they get their first child, the couple usually get a flat.'

SPEAKING FOR RELATIVES

The custom of 'speaking for' relatives (as it is called) is backed up by a body of sentiment in each street and block. Many people in them have got places for kindred – special local inquiries, in places that were as far as we could discover fairly typical, showed that in one street containing 59 households, 38 had relatives in other households; in one block of buildings containing 52 households, 28 had relatives in it; in another block, with 176 households, 64 had relatives. What people have done for themselves they approve of others doing also. The local residents all know that Mrs Brown, say, wants a place for her daughter, and, if a house falls empty, their view is that she should get it in preference to any outsider. The rent collector or, for buildings, the superintendent, who may themselves have lifelong acquaintance with the neighbourhood, do not lightly disregard this feeling. Being well aware of local opinion, they protect themselves from criticism by conforming with the unwritten code, and even persuade others to do likewise. One agent allowed Mr and Mrs Meadows to move in to the house next door to the husband's parents when the previous tenant died.

'He said "You can have it, but there are lots of others in the street who want rooms and if I were you I'd let the top half to avoid animosity." There were quite a lot of daughters and sons in the street wanting a place, so that's what we did. We let the upstairs to a girl who'd just got married and whose mother lives at 39. When they got the upstairs and we got the downstairs, there wasn't any bad feeling – not that I know of, anyway – because the place had been taken over by two families who'd lived here for years.'

The two Councils already own nearly a third of the dwellings in the borough and are increasing their share every year.[1] They select their tenants by different methods. They give preference to 'slum' dwellers and people whose need is judged greatest, not on the grounds of a person's family relationships. The whole complex, informal, intimate, and chancy network of relative 'speaking for' relative spreads

1. By the beginning of 1962 they owned nearly half.

only to the doors of the Town Hall. Inside, and at County Hall, 'speaking for' is not time-hallowed custom, it is nepotism. Although any day you can see a large round mother standing with her slim and anxious daughter behind her at the counter of the Housing Department, in this sphere her voice cannot gain priority for her children. Kindly administrators do their best to see that members of families get rehoused close together. But it is much rarer for Council tenants to be clustered in families, for the mother has none of the special influence with the local authorities that she does with the private rent collectors.

We have, in this chapter, discussed the interaction of kinship and housing administration. It is a complicated story. A neighbour dies, a family moves upon change of job, Mum bumps into a friend in the pub, the collector remembers you as a child, your home is pronounced a slum, a son has tuberculosis – chance often seems to be the distributor of houses. But, despite the galaxy of accident, there is, as we have seen, a tendency for residence to be matrilocal. This residential pattern suggests the possibility of a close tie between mother and daughter, which will be further considered in the next chapter.

Bethnal Green suffers from a serious housing shortage. In time, we can hope, it will be much less acute than it is now, so that residence will be less accident and more choice. What would happen then to matrilocality? We could not get a simple answer to such a hypothetical question. In Bethnal Green there is most certainly no explicit rule, formal or informal, as there is in some other societies, that couples should live near to the wife's parents. People's views about living near to parents are not their sole thought; their views about bathrooms and hot water, flats and gardens, also count. We can only give our opinion, formed in the course of numerous long discussions, about what would happen. Relieving the shortage of houses would, we believe, work in two opposite ways. Fewer married daughters would share with their parents once the necessity were removed; some daughters who regretfully took a house near their mothers merely to take advantage of family influence would seize the opportunity to move farther away. On the other hand, many daughters who at present live with parents would want to continue to live near them and more of the daughters living at a distance not from choice would move closer to them. This second group would, we believe, outnumber the first: the general preference in this district is, as we have said, the same as that found by Sheldon in Wolverhampton.

3

MOTHERS AND DAUGHTERS

WE shall now follow up the hint in the last chapter about
the tie between mothers and daughters, and consider some
aspects of the interaction between them. We shall start with
an example which shows how much their lives are sometimes woven together.

Mr and Mrs Wilkins live with their two children on the
ground floor of Tabernacle Buildings, about which he says,
'I suppose the buildings in Bethnal Green aren't all that
good, but we don't look on this as a pile of stones. It isn't the
buildings that matter. We like the people here.' For them,
'the people' means first and foremost the relatives. One of
the wife's sisters, Joyce, lives with her husband and children
in the same block, another of her sisters, Joan, and one of
the husband's brothers in the same turning, and her mother
and father in another nearby street. Mrs Wilkins is in and
out of her mother's all day. She shops with her in the morning and goes round there for a cup of tea in the afternoon.
'Then any time during the day, if I want a bit of salt or
something like that, I go round to Mum to get it and have
a bit of a chat while I'm there.' If the children have anything wrong with them, 'I usually go round to my Mum and
have a little chat. If she thinks it's serious enough I'll take
him to the doctor.' Her mother looked after Marilyn, the
oldest child, for nearly three years. 'She's always had her
when I worked; I worked from when she was just a little
baby until I was past six months with Billy. Oh, she's all
for our Mum. She's got her own mates over there and still
plays there all the time. Mum looks after my girl pretty
good. When she comes in, I say "Have you had your tea?",
and she says as often as not, "I've had it at Nan's."'

Mrs Wilkins, and her husband for that matter, also see
her two sisters frequently. Joyce and her husband happened

44

to walk by during the interview and stopped to chat through
the open window. The two husbands talked about a horse
and cart that some man in the street was going to buy, and
Joyce said something about bringing down a dress which
Joan's little girl had grown out of. As she left, Joyce called
back about Joan's baby: 'Isn't the baby getting fat?' Joyce
is the one who runs the 'family club' (of which there are
many in Bethnal Green): she collects 2s. 6d. a week from
the members who can draw out whenever they need to,
which is usually at Christmas. Mrs Wilkins's parents are in
it, all the sisters and their husbands, and two brothers. 'Even
the children are in it. Apart from the family there's only
one outsider,' said Mr Wilkins, 'a fellow I've worked with
for years. I've belonged to one of these clubs all my life.
Before I got married I belonged to my father's, and when I
got married, I joined Joyce's.'

Mrs Wilkins is in one or two important ways like many
other women we interviewed. She lives near her mother,
and, as we know from the last chapter, this is not uncommon. She also sees a great deal of her, and this again is not
uncommon. We asked all our informants who had parents
alive how long before the interview they had last seen them.
Table 6 shows the proportion of married women, and married men, who had seen their parents within the previous
twenty-four hours. Distance is here ignored, parents being
included wherever they live, whether they are in East London or not.

Over half the married women saw their mothers within the
previous twenty-four hours and 80 per cent of them within
the previous week. This was more than they saw their fathers
or the married men saw of either of their parents. We also
inquired of the people in the marriage sample *how often* they
saw their parents and other relatives: from this it appeared
that, on average, the wives saw their mothers about four
times a week.

These quantitative measures underline the significance of
the mother-daughter relationship. But the number of contacts is less important than their content. To convey some

TABLE 6: Contacts of Married Men and Women with Parents

(General sample – married people only)

	Fathers		Mothers	
	Number with father alive	Percentage of those with father alive who saw him in previous twenty-four hours	Number with mother alive	Percentage of those with mother alive who saw her in previous twenty-four hours
Men	116	30%	163	31%
Women	100	48%	155	55%

indication of what really goes on between the two people, we have to fall back on the accounts given to us in our interviews and order the impressions left upon us by the people to whom we have talked. The accounts are examples, no more. The marriage sample of forty-five couples was not only small to begin with but is, for the purpose of this chapter, made smaller because not all of the wives had mothers whom they could see. The mothers of eleven of them were dead, and seven were living in Eire, the North of England, or at such a distance outside London that frequent contact was difficult. In the main we here speak of the remaining twenty-seven wives, of whom fifteen saw their mothers at least once a day; the other eleven at least once and usually several times in the week. The remaining one, Mrs Saville, was exceptional in that she had, in defiance of local convention, not only quarrelled but broken off relations with her mother. She is referred to again.

THE WIFE'S DAY

We asked the wives to give us brief diaries of their days. Mum was rarely absent. Mrs Cole, for instance, lives in the same street as her mother, together with her husband and three children, two of them under five, the other at school.

'After breakfast I bath the baby and sweep the kitchen, and wash up. Then I go up the road shopping with Mum, Greta (one of the wife's married sisters who also has a child), and the three children. After dinner I clean up and then round about 2 o'clock I go out for a walk if it's fine with Mum and Greta and the children. I come back at about a quarter to four to be in time for Janice when she gets back from school. She calls in at Mum's on her way home just to see if I'm there. This is an ordinary day. If anything goes wrong and I'm in any trouble I always go running round to Mum's.'

And so it went on – 'My Mum comes round at about 3.15 – she comes round regularly at that time to spend the afternoon'; 'Mum's always popping in here – twelve times a day I should say'; 'Then my Mum and I collect Stephen from the school and go back to her place for tea'; 'We usually have dinner round at her place'; 'She's always popping in here'; 'We've got four keys – one for each of us, one for Mum, and one for Mary. That's so they can come in any time they like.' 'Popping in' for a chat and a cup of tea is the routine of normal life.

These accounts put a new light on the ordinary idea of the household. People live together and eat together – they are considered to be in the same household. But what if they spend a good part of the day and eat (or at least drink tea) regularly in someone else's household? The households are then to some extent merged. This is most obvious where two families actually live in the same house. 'When my husband's home in the evenings we eat separate. But in the day we usually have our meals with Mum, or she comes up with us.' This may also happen with households not under the same roof at all. One woman lives five minutes away yet 'I have dinner with Mum, so that leaves me free to do my housework and get my husband his meal in the evening.' The daily lives of many women are not confined to the places where they sleep; they are spread over two or more households, in each of which they regularly spend part of their time. This mixing up of domestic arrangements has been noticed before, by Sheldon in the Wolverhampton study already quoted. Referring to old people, he says:

'In at least 40 per cent of cases they must be regarded as part of a family group, the ramifications of which bear little or no relation to architectural limitations . . .'[1]

The kind of 'family group' of which Sheldon speaks is certainly as much a reality in Bethnal Green as in Wolverhampton. It most commonly consists of a small cluster of families, that is, the families of marriage of the daughters and their common family of origin, and it is made up in the main of the three generations of grandparents, parents, and grandchildren. When people talk about 'the family', it is very often this combination of the two sorts of family which they have in mind, and since it is such an important grouping in their day-to-day lives, it deserves a name of its own. We propose to adopt the anthropologists' term, 'extended family', when we want to refer to a combination of families who to some large degree form one domestic unit.

Not all the members of an extended family necessarily live close together. But the nearer they are to their mothers, the easier it is for daughters to pass back and forth. If we go by the same measure of contact that we have used before, we find in Table 7, as we would expect, that the nearer women do on the whole see more of their mothers.

TABLE 7: Contacts of Women According to
Distance of Mothers

*(General sample – 133 married women with mothers alive
and not in the same dwelling)*

Residence of mother	Number of married women	Women who saw their mother in previous twenty-four hours
Same street or block of flats	23	23
Elsewhere in Bethnal Green	49	33
Adjacent borough	25	4
Elsewhere	36	3

1. Sheldon, J. H. op. cit., p. 156.

The mother is the head and centre of the extended family, her home its meeting place. 'Mum's is the family rendezvous,' as one wife said. Her daughters congregate at the mother's, visiting her more often than she visits any one of them: 68 per cent of married women last saw their mother at her home, and only 27 per cent at their own. When there, they quite often see their other sisters, and brothers too, particularly if they are still living at home, but even if they live elsewhere, the sisters may call there at the usual time in the afternoon for a cup of tea, or just happen to drop in for a chat on their way to the shops. Regular weekly meetings often supplement the day-to-day visiting.

'All my family', said Mrs Shipway, 'gather at Mum's every Saturday afternoon. We sit jawing, and get amused with the children when all of them get together, play cards, and listen to the wireless. No one leaves until tenish at night. It always happens on a Saturday.'

In addition to the weekly meetings there are special family gatherings at the mother's house for birthdays and wedding anniversaries, Mum's own birthday being one of the occasions of the year. In one family our informant, as the eldest sister, who had taken it upon herself to make the arrangements for the birthday, explained the meaning of the event.

'My Dad died when I was fourteen. Mum was a brick. Even if we never had shoes on our feet, we always had good grub. She always kept a good table. I'm going to get a special party together for next year when Mum is eighty. Since we've had a family of our own, we realize how Mum's worked for us in the past.'

It almost goes without saying that where Mum plays so large a part in the lives of her descendants, she should be honoured for what she does. The very word, and the warmth with which it is uttered, somehow conveys the respect in which she is held. Since her status as 'Mum' is so high, it is derogatory to call her by any other name. Mrs Gould, for one, thinks the use of any mere Christian name a disgusting example of the 'American' way of doing things.

'It's terrible, it doesn't sound right, it doesn't make the woman feel responsible for her home duties. She'll think "I don't need to bother – this is not a home." It sounds like a distant relation, but "Mum" puts a woman on a pedestal where she should be.'

Most women take it for granted (however inappropriate the image) that this is where Mum belongs – 'on a pedestal'. 'I'm very devoted to Mum, of course, that's understood with mothers and daughters,' says Mrs Warner and, like many others, leaves it at that, as a statement of the obvious, hardly worth making.

EXCHANGE OF SERVICES

The sentiment is so strong partly because the mothers, as well as acting as the organizers of social life, perform so many important services for their daughters. We shall now consider some of these services, starting with the help given at child-birth. It is natural that at this time the daughter should draw on the knowledge of her mother who has been through it all before. When is she to stop work? What clothes is she to make? What is she to eat, and not eat? Should she have the baby at home or in hospital? Should she do the exercises advised by the 'welfare'? What is to happen to the home whilst she is confined? All her doubts, fears, and hopes are discussed with the person who is the close companion of her daily life.

When the confinement comes, someone else has to look after the home while the wife is in bed. All the forty-five couples in the marriage sample had at least two children under fifteen. At the last birth, about which we inquired in most detail, there was therefore at least one other child, as well as a husband, to provide for. The child had to be looked after, food bought, meals cooked, clothes washed, and preparations made for the care of the new baby. We know from a previous national survey that in this emergency the family usually gets the support it needs from relatives; Home Helps from public authorities have not displaced the kindred. For the country as a whole the Population Investigation

Committee, acting with the Royal College of Obstetricians and Gynaecologists, reported that:

> Relatives were by far the most important source of help at child-birth. They gave domestic assistance to 83 per cent of those who were helped. Their help was more frequently given to the poorer women, the black-coated, manual, and agricultural workers' wives.[1]

Bethnal Green is, in this respect, like the nation. As Mrs Banks said, 'Strangers are all right but you prefer your own every time.' Only one wife, with her mother dead, made arrangements for a Home Help. 'But Lennie was born on a Friday and the Home Help doesn't come over the week-end. By the time Monday came you could say the worst was over, so we didn't bother to have her after all. On the Monday my husband went to the manager of the firm where he worked and he said he could have a week off. So he had the week off from work and looked after the home and the children.'

The wife's mother was usually the great standby. But some wives had no mothers they could call on. Seven of them were dead, four too old and infirm to be able to do much, five lived far away, in Eire or in the North of England, and although one of them came down from Liverpool she was not able to stay for more than the first few days. Out of the other twenty-eight mothers,[2] eighteen took over the main responsibility for their daughters' homes while they were in bed, either coming in to stay every day or taking the other children away to live with them; seven gave some substantial assistance, although not having the main responsibility; and three did nothing.

Two families – the Warners and the Sopers – can illustrate what was done by the first group. Mrs Warner's eldest girl

1. *Maternity in Great Britain*, p. 183.
2. The total number accounted for is only forty-four instead of forty-five because in one family the older child was also in hospital, ill, at the time, and the husband looked after himself. The number of mothers dead at the time of their daughter's confinement was four less than at the time of interview, owing to the difference between the dates.

went to stay with her grandmother for a fortnight and her husband slept and had all his meals there, including breakfast. 'As a matter of fact, while I was in hospital my husband and father decorated the kitchen out for me. My mother did all the work while I was away, and then when I came out of hospital, she did all my shopping for a few days after I came home. While I was in hospital Mum went out and bought all the things we needed for the baby, like the pram and the bath. I'd talked it over beforehand with her like, and told her what to get.' Mrs Soper's story was much the same. Her mother lives on a housing estate at Harold Hill. 'Alfie went down to stay with my Mum when I had Johnny. Then Mum came up here the day before I was coming out of hospital and sort of got the place cleaned up. She was here the day I came out and stayed the next day. Then she went home.'

Mrs Robbins can stand for the second group of seven. One of her sisters who lived very close had the eldest child to stay with her. 'Another sister got my errands for me, and my mother came in and did a lot of the cooking. My husband did some of the cooking too. Being on shift work, he was at home in the daytime sometimes, and he was able to give a hand.'

The three mothers not conforming to rule – the mothers of Mrs Saville, Mrs Glass, and Mrs Merton – were all the more interesting for that.

(1) Mrs Saville was one of the two who had quarrelled. Her mother, who was only forty-seven, 'has a boy of her own only ten months older than ours. Our boy's bigger than hers, although he's younger. They had a bit of a sort-out up the street, and that started the trouble between us.' The fact that her own mother was still in the same phase of life as her daughter had somehow made it impossible for her to perform the usual role. Even before the quarrel, almost from the beginning of her married life, Mrs Saville had leaned more on mother-in-law than on mother. She recognized how unusual this was. 'His Mum's always been more like my Mum should, you know what I mean?'

(2) Mrs Glass, the second of the three, was resentful that

her youngest sister, still living with her mother, took so much of her attention. 'Mum's all for my sister. She looks after her baby so that she can go out to work. She's never offered to look after ours. I ain't in her good books at all.' She too added the comment, attributed to her husband, that 'He was really surprised at my Mum not coming round.'

(3) Between Mrs Merton and her mother, the third in this group, there had been no open quarrel. The mother had five single children still living with her, the youngest being nine, and was busy looking after them all. On the other hand, the husband's mother was a widow, living alone and very keen to help. He was intending to go to her for his own meals, and preferred that his older boy should stay there, so that he would be able to eat with him. Both Mrs Merton and Mrs Saville had, on this occasion at any rate, substituted mother-in-law for mother.

OTHER AID FOR THE WIFE

Mothers were as much on the scene after the birth of children as they were at the confinement itself. Wives can obtain help from other quarters. The State has established a welfare service of doctors, clinics, and health visitors, which has an advisory as well as a purely medical function. But the arrival of the expert has not led to the banishment of the grandmother. She has an advantage over the men of the service in that she is a woman, and over its female members, who are often unmarried, in that she has been a mother herself. The daughter's very existence demonstrates that she knows what she is talking about. 'It was on her advice at the beginning', said Mrs Sykes, 'that I knew what to do. I hadn't had any children before and she had.'

When the wife gets contradictory advice from the welfare clinic and from her Mum, she usually listens to the person she trusts most – Mrs Banton being an example.

'I take more notice of my Mum than I do of the welfare. She's had eight and we're all right. Experience speaks for itself, more or less, doesn't it? If you're living near your mother, you don't really need that advice. You've got more confidence in your mother than you would have in the advice they'd give you. When I was in the hospital they taught me how to bath him – you're supposed to lay him out on your knees on a towel. But as soon as I got home, Mum said "Don't bother with doing it like that. Just put him in the water and wash him." Then they said that I ought to always bath him in the morning, but Mum said, "You bath him in the evening. He'll sleep better then." '

So is Mrs Banks:

'I didn't pay much attention to what they said at the clinic and I stopped taking the baby when he caught cold after the undressing up there. I go by what Mum tells me. It's too fussy and fandangled up there. I'd rather take old-fashioned advice by experience.'

And so is Mrs Power:

'Before I had the baby, I used to say "My baby won't have a dummy." And then when I left the hospital they said he'd got a little gripe – you know, his little tummy – and they told me to give him some gripe-water. When I came home with him, he was so tiny, to try and get a spoonful of gripe-water in his mouth would have choked him. My Mum said there was only one way to give him the gripe-water and that was on a dummy. So she went out and bought a dummy and we dipped it in the gripe-water and that was it – we had a good baby.'

The wife's dependence for help on her kin, and especially upon her mother, does not end with the confinement and its aftermath. Whatever the emergency, and whether her need is big or small, the wife looks to her mother for advice and for aid. We have explained, in the last chapter, how the mother helps her daughter to find a house. What if she goes out to work? Since all the wives had young children, they were at the stage of life when it is least easy to combine work and home; and in fact only nineteen of the forty-five were in paid employment. The eight with part-time work arranged their hours so that they fitted in with the needs of their children. Part-time work is plentiful in Bethnal Green, both in the small local factories and in the tens of thousands of offices which have to be cleaned in the nearby City, and women are therefore less in need of help from relatives than they would be in many other places. Two wives, engaged in their own homes as out-workers for firms of tailors, had their children by their side.

Of the remaining nine wives in full-time work, seven had to entrust their children to other people for at least part of the day; and six of these relied on their relatives. An extreme example is Mrs Sykes, whose eldest daughter actually lives with her grandmother.

'Brenda lives with my mother now. Well she's got the room and we haven't. I see Mum every morning before I go off to work. You see, the other children go round there before they go to school. I give them their breakfast, then when I go off to work I leave them at Mum's. They go round to her again after school.'

Mrs Trimble is more usual. Both her children are at school but have mid-day dinner and tea with their grandmother. Mrs Trimble calls there every morning on her way to work, and leaves some food for the children's meals. Since there is no one at home during the day, Mum also 'holds my rent book and pays the rent man for me'.

We also asked about illness. Rather to our surprise, nearly half the wives had not at any time been ill enough to take to their beds. The question was sometimes greeted with derisory laughter. 'No, I never go to bed. When I'm feeling ill I just sit in a chair. I can't afford to lay in bed.' As a rule it was only for major illnesses that they retired to bed, or sometimes to hospital. A third of the twenty-four wives who had done this relied mainly on older children and husbands to keep their homes going. Four of the other sixteen wives had parents who were either dead or far away, in Eire or Manchester, and these called upon neighbours or friends. The remaining twelve wives were assisted by relatives, with their own mothers again prominent.

'I had to go into hospital suddenly,' said Mrs Soper. 'My sister-in-law upstairs looked after the children until my mother got here. She stayed on and looked after my husband and the little boy and the baby until I got back. I was ever so homesick.'

There is also cooperation on the more ordinary occasions of life. The wife, shall we say, wants to go out shopping and it is too tiring to take the baby – 'If I want to go up the shops or to the launderette in the morning, Mum has him for an hour or so.' When she wants to go out in the evening to the cinema with her husband, she does not have to look far for a 'baby-sitter' – 'Mum doesn't come round here and sit in with the kiddies. We take them round to her place and they stay there while we're out at the pictures.' She may not have enough laundry of her own for the 'bag-wash' – 'I take my washing round to Mum every week. She sends it to the bag-wash in the same bag as hers. She usually dries it out when it comes back.' And so it goes on – the daughter's labours are in a hundred little ways shared with the older woman whose days of child-bearing (but not of child-rearing) are over. When the time comes for the mother to need assistance, the daughter reciprocates, as reported elsewhere,[1] by returning the care which she has herself received.

THE REPRESENTATIVE OF TRADITION

We would not be right to leave the impression that the course of relations always runs smooth. Some conflict between the generations is common; except in degree, nearly all families are in this alike. The mothers represent tradition. They hold to religion and to the old ways more tenaciously than their children, and may be up against the more modern ideas learnt by the wives, and even more by the husbands, from sources outside the family. The husbands, we found, were the main upholders of progress against the claims of tradition. Mr Meadows, for example, was a strong ally of the welfare clinic, who wanted his wife to follow its teaching rather than his mother-in-law's. He criticized mothers in general because 'They go by the old things – they're more old-fashioned. I know she's always saying when we were young we used to do this, that, and the other.' With this encouragement, his wife was unusual enough to plump for the clinic.

There is the same conflict over churching. On this, most of the wives were clearly under maternal influence. Both

1. By Townsend, P. *The Family Life of Old People.*

regular churchgoers, a small minority, and irregular attenders alike thought they should go to church as soon as possible after the confinement, for the service whose formal
purpose is thanksgiving for the birth of the child.

'It's the Mums. It's not that I actually believe in it, but I'd get
an uneasy feeling if I didn't do it. You don't like to break tradition.'

'I heard about it when I was little. My mother believed in it,
but not like some mothers. She's not one who thinks you shouldn't
go out until you've been churched. It's more of a tradition really,
isn't it, getting churched?'

The idea still lingers on that childbirth has in some way
made the mother unclean. Many wives, even while talking
about superstition, still believe it wrong to go out in public
until the service is over.

'It's a very old-fashioned custom. It's superstition really. It's
supposed to be unlucky if you go out before you're churched.'

'My mother believes it. She's superstitious like that. I don't
believe it really but I did stay in for three or four days after I got
back and before I got churched.'

Husbands were sometimes sarcastic about their wives' un-
thinking acceptance of maternal attitudes. When his wife
said of churching 'It's your religion, isn't it? I mean you've
got to do it', Mr Jeffreys added 'Your Mum's done it – you
do it. They're all the same.' When Mrs Robbins, explaining
the custom, said 'It's after you've had the baby. You go
and give thanks to God that you're safe and all that. It's just
a matter of form, really,' her husband broke in to remark,
'Because your mother done it, you mean.' But however op-
posed the husbands may be, however much they feel the
practice is old-fashioned, on this score the wives continue to
follow tradition. Out of the forty-five wives in the marriage
sample, all except four were churched after the birth of their
last child.

The two generations may also disagree, as the children
get older, about discipline. Here in Bethnal Green we can
observe what anthropologists have noticed in many places.

The parents are in authority over the children. Theirs is the responsibility for teaching them the duties and rights, skills and manners, which will fit them to take their place as adult members of society, theirs in some measure the power to command obedience. Parents cannot treat their children as equals. But grandparents are not primarily responsible for teaching right behaviour. They do not need to exert as much authority. By being more easy-going, they can supply the children with another model of what adults are like. As one anthropologist put it, the relationship between grandparents and grandchildren is one 'of friendly familiarity and almost of social equality'.

In general also, in Africa as elsewhere, grandparents are much more indulgent towards their grandchildren than are parents to their children. A child who feels that he is being treated with severity by his father may appeal to his father's father. The grandparents are the persons above all others who can interfere in the relations between parents and children.[1]

The description certainly applies to Bethnal Green. Here are two examples. In one home we conducted part of the interview with Mr Cole alone while his wife was in the kitchen. Janice, his ten-year-old daughter, sat by his side listening, with a rather bored expression on her face, to all the talk. Then when we came to the questions about grandparents, Janice suddenly became very excited and rushed off into the kitchen to tell her mother that the man was asking about 'Nan'. When she returned, she burst out with a series of superlatives about her maternal grandmother. 'Good old Nanny, she's my pal. She's a good old girl.' When asked whether this granny was strict with her, she said gleefully, 'No, she was strict to Mummy when she was a little girl. She's not strict to us' – this last with a note almost of triumph in her voice. The husband explained, rather sheepishly, that 'they both like their gran'.

1. Radcliffe-Brown, A. R. Intro. to *African Systems of Kinship and Marriage*, p. 28. In some primitive societies the bond between grandparents and grandchildren is such as to produce what has been called the 'merging of alternate generations'. ibid. pp. 29–31.

In the Tawney family the maternal grandfather was more of the favourite. The parents and children sometimes stayed the night with him. 'They used to say to him, "Come on, come on to bed, Dad." And he used to undress – at eight o'clock in the evening – and go to bed with them to get them to sleep. He'd get up pretending to use the bucket when he thought they were asleep, but if they weren't, they'd say: "What is it, Dad?" and he'd say "Nothing. I'm just using the bucket. I'm coming back to bed."'

Sometimes the two sets of grandparents competed with each other for the affections of their grandchildren. 'His mother', said one woman, 'never had a girl herself and always wanted a grand-daughter. She's very fond of her. Mum dotes on her too. One won't be outdone by the other. If one buys her something the other must try and get one better. Mum started a bank book for her. She wanted to put £50 in. She wants to give her everything, but I said "no". I wouldn't let her put more than £10 in the bank for her.' In another family the competition was between 'Big Nanny', as the wife's mother was called, and 'Television Nanny', the title given to the husband's mother as the first of the relatives to get a set.

The grandchildren are the blood descendants of both sets of grandparents, and in some measure belong to, and form a link between, the two families of origin. But once again we were struck by the paramountcy of the wife's mother. On the whole, the grandchildren saw more of her than of the husband's mother. The eldest grandchild, in the thirty families with grandparents alive on both sides, saw the maternal grandmother 3.8 times a week, on average, and the paternal grandmother only 1.8 times a week. Like wives, like children. When the wives went to see their mothers they took the children with them. When they went on a visit to someone else, they arranged for the children to call in at their Mum's for tea after school. The children more often received weekly pocket-money from the maternal grandparents. But though the wife's mother predominated, she did not do so to the exclusion of the husband's mother. In many families it was the regular practice for the husband to take the children round to his parents on a Sunday; others lived closer to the husband's parents and it was easier for the children to drop in on them.

Naturally enough, the parents did not always approve of the familiarity between their parents and their children. They felt the older generation were too indulgent. 'My mother', said Mrs Jones, 'spoils her terrible. She's much easier than she was with us. The things she lets her do!' 'The grandparents like to give them all their own way, that's the trouble,' said Mrs Madge. Mrs Power remarked of her husband's mother, 'I think she spoils them because she's got no other grandchildren. What makes it worse is that they're girls – she always wanted a girl herself, but she got six boys.' The first grandchild to be born was more likely than later arrivals to have attention and gifts lavished upon him. 'She spoils him a lot. He's the first grandchild after all.' 'His mother gave the shawl and lots of clothes for the baby. She gave a lot because it was her first grandchild, you see.'

This was almost the only subject on which Mrs Banton disagreed, though only mildly, with her mother. 'She sticks up for Dickie all the time. The other night we wanted to take him over the park with us and the baby, but he said he didn't want to come. He said he was tired. Mum said "He don't want to come. Let him stay. He's all right here." If he's naughty she always sticks up for him. She loves him.'

So we can, to conclude this chapter, see that some wives, and more husbands, do not agree with Mum all the time. But even if they resent her interference, she is a presence in their lives. The character of a kinship system is shown by the relationships which it emphasizes. Sometimes it is (in addition to that between husband and wife) the relationship between father and son, sometimes between siblings, sometimes uncle and nephew. Here in Bethnal Green, the relationship stressed, alongside that of marriage, is between mother and daughter.

The woman is not cut off from her daughter by marriage. While in one way she has lost her to her new son-in-law, in another way she has recovered her as a daughter. Previous crises in the life of the family, beginning of school and start of work, have withdrawn daughter as well as son from the mother's home. Both made school-friends and work-friends of their own age from outside the family. When daughters, almost as much as sons, absorbed themselves in the display and adventure of adolescence, excitement lay in the life of workplace and club, street and gang, cinema and holiday camp. As long as she was working in a man's world the daughter behaved in many ways like a man, clocking on at a factory like her brother and earning her own money to spend as she chose. But when she marries, and even more when she leaves work to have children, she returns to the woman's world, and to her mother. Marriage divides the sexes into their distinctive roles, and so strengthens the relationship between the daughter and the mother who has been through it all before. The old proverb applies:

> My son's a son till he gets him a wife,
> My daughter's a daughter all her life.

The daughter continues to live near her mother. She is a member of her extended family. She receives advice and support from her in the great personal crises and on the small domestic occasions. They share so much and give such help to each other because, in their women's world, they have the same functions of caring for home and bringing up children.

4

HUSBANDS AND MOTHERS

W E have already said enough to suggest what a characteristic conflict is likely to be in Bethnal Green – the result of stressing the mother-daughter tie being that there is an inherent tension between the husband and his mother-in-law. Both mother and husband have claims on the loyalty and affections of the same person, and, if the marriage is to reach stability, they have to adjust these claims by coming to terms with each other.

Matrimony is a relationship of social groups as well as individuals, the two principal partners representing the two 'sides' from which they come. The twofold division which gives rise to the need for such far-reaching adjustments can be well observed at any wedding in Bethnal Green; and since observation can here supplement interviews, we start by describing one of them, between Sylvia Hanbury and Harry Buxton, she from the Bow end of Bethnal Green and he a docker from Shadwell.

The reception was held at the bride's home. After the wedding in the late afternoon, the bride and groom moved off from the church in their hired Rolls Royce and the wedding guests followed in smaller cars. Once arrived in Mr Hanbury's front room, most of the guests stood about rather stiffly, holding glasses of beer and sniffing the pickled onions. The Buxtons, that is the bridegroom's family, were grouped by the window looking disdainfully at the chipped china dogs on the mantelpiece, the worn linoleum on the floor, and the pictures of country scenes which did not quite conceal the damp patches on the wall-paper. Mrs Alice Buxton, the mother, said, 'I don't know whether I'm the bride or not. I'm shaking like a leaf.' Mr Hanbury, with a slightly forced joviality, called out for the first toast, and they all turned with raised glasses of beer to the smiling bride and bridegroom, who were standing behind the small table by the fireplace on which towered the tiered wedding cake. 'They must have got Mowlems to put that up,' said one of the Buxtons when the toast was over.

The thirty-two guests squeezed down at the cramped tables for the wedding breakfast of ham and tongue, salad and pickles, trifle and jelly, washed down with ale and Guinness. The heat became greater, the faces more flushed and the talk louder. After an hour, the meal and toasts over, the telegrams read, the trestle tables were cleared and stacked away. Sylvia and Harry concentrated on trying to bring the two families together. They were not to go off to their honeymoon – a three-day stay at Clacton – until the next morning. In Bethnal Green, where they were born and bred, couples do not fly off to a honeymoon when the first reception is over. 'I'm going to stay till the very end, that's if we ever get away. We haven't actually booked,' said Sylvia, 'I wouldn't miss a minute of it.'

Harry took off his new jacket and carried a tray of drinks around the by now smoky room. Before long he anxiously asked his wife's grandmother, who was sitting close to the fire, 'It's going very well, isn't it, Gran? Everybody's mucking in, I mean, you can't tell which side is which, can you?'

At nine o'clock the men decided to go over to the pub, where they all contributed a £1 a head 'whip' for the purchase of drinks. Soon the wedding party filled the saloon bar of the City of Paris, where it had been joined by some of Sylvia's and Harry's workmates; not being relatives, they were not invited to the reception, but they dropped in to the pub 'to wish you luck'. Sylvia's brother, Jack, on his way to the 'Gents' stopped for a word with some friends in the other bar. 'Didn't Sylvie look lovely?' said a bent old woman, a neighbour from along the street who said she had been present when Sylvia was born; she had stood at her doorway that afternoon, waiting excitedly for the bride and groom to come back from the church in the Rolls. 'How's it going, Jack?' asked a red-faced man who pressed Jack into having a drink with him. 'All right,' Jack said, 'very well, really. But they're a funny lot. Greedy too. You should have seen the drink they put away this afternoon.' He gave the bar-counter an authoritative rap. 'It won't last, if you ask me. Sylvie'll be back home within a week.'

When the pub closed some of the relatives living in Stepney, Dagenham, or East Ham went home, the others returned to the Hanburys', and many newcomers arrived. Two men could be heard talking about the bride's mother. 'She's a funny woman,' one of them emphatically declared. 'I told her off this afternoon when she said she was tired. "Of course you're tired," I told her straight, "we're all bleeding tired." She didn't take no notice though. Like water off a duck's back.'

'She *is* a funny woman,' the younger man answered seriously. As the husband of one of the bride's sisters, he was talking about his mother-in-law. 'I've tried, Bert, I've tried ever since we got married, to be friends with her, but we just don't seem to get on.'

'To tell you the truth, Frank,' the other leaned forward conspiratorially, 'I don't think I ever could get on with that woman. Anyway,' he added with an air of finality, 'you married Ethel, didn't you? You didn't marry her bleeding family.' Despite these sentiments, the two of them rejoined the party and soon all of them including the two mothers, were dancing and laughing around the room together, in the early hours of the morning, one family indistinguishable from the other.

THE TRIANGLE OF ADULT LIFE

The great triangle of childhood is mother-father-child; in Bethnal Green the great triangle of adult life is Mum-wife-husband. In this three-cornered relationship the tension is between Harry Buxton and the mother of the girl into whose family he has married.

Some husbands we interviewed were more articulate about it than others. 'My wife wants to stay near her mother,' said one outspoken husband. 'For myself, I've got

nothing against my mother-in-law – she's always been very
good to me – but I'd like to get as far away from her as I
possibly can.' Mr Warner said, pointedly, in his wife's presence, 'Some people are too close to their mothers, if you
ask me. They ought to stand on their own feet a bit more.'
Mr Marris told us that although he and his wife had moved
out to a flat at Enfield when they first married, she insisted
on coming back to live with Mum when her first baby was
due. 'There was a difference of opinion over it,' he said, 'she
wanted to come back to her Mum and I didn't.'

The reasons for such an attitude become apparent if one
considers the experience of some other marriages. 'I know
she's your mother,' one man told his wife, 'but she sometimes forgets I'm your husband.' 'My sisters are married
but they're not really married, if you know what I mean,'
another informant said. 'When they finish work they go
straight round to Mum's and don't get home till 9.30 or 10
at night.' Mrs Warner, to instance another wife, was so identified with her mother that it turned out that when she said
'us' during the interview she meant Mum and her, not her
husband and herself: '*We* see so-and-so' meant 'I see them
at Mum's.' Husbands so excluded from the feminine circle
can be understood if they feel resentful of Mum's influence.

The tension is sharpest when the couple actually live with
the wife's parents. 'My mother-in-law isn't a bad old stick,'
said Mr White, 'but it's not easy. My wife has to side with
her Mum every time there's a difference, and I have to side
with my wife. Say I put the radiogram on, she thinks it's too
loud and comes in with a headache. Or I come in and bang
the door or something like that. From time to time I get
fidgety too, and arguments start up over the silliest little
things.'

Mr and Mrs Jones and their three children live in the top
half of a two-storey terraced house near Cambridge Heath
Road; downstairs are Mrs Jones's parents. During the day
the wife often pops down to her mother and relies on her to
help with the children. During the evening the cold war
between Mr Jones and his mother-in-law is resumed.

'The old man's not so bad,' says Mr Jones, 'but I don't get on with her mother, that's the truth. She's always going on about something – walking about down there effing and blinding about what I've done and what I haven't done. Of course, we all eff and blind sometimes – I daresay you do it sometimes, too – but I don't like the children to hear it.'

To say that the relationship between husband and mother-in-law is a source of tension does not mean, of course, that every husband is as bitter as Mr Jones. Open hostility is rare, simply because it is too uncomfortable for all concerned. The possibility of conflict is always there, the tension implicit in the triangle can seldom be completely resolved, but some form of adjustment, some equilibrium, is usually achieved, in Bethnal Green as elsewhere. 'Tensions and possibilities of conflict exist in all systems,' as Radcliffe-Brown has pointed out. 'For a system to work efficiently it must provide methods of limiting, controlling, or resolving such conflicts or tensions.'[1]

EASING THE STRAIN

How is the triangle of forces dealt with in Bethnal Green? One possibility is for the wife to abandon her mother in favour of her husband and desert her old family for her new. Mr and Mrs Mann, when we interviewed them, were in process of choosing this way out aided by an L.C.C. 'slum clearance' scheme, and their story, though far from typical, illustrates this one solution.

After the wedding they lived with her parents. 'It was difficult then,' said Mrs Mann. 'We were all on top of each other.' Her mother spoke to her collector and 'four months after he offered us this place. We were in two minds about coming here – it's a terrible place. But my husband said anything to get on our own, so we took it.' When interviewed they had been living there for eighteen months, and since Mrs Mann had stopped work a couple of months before the

1. Radcliffe-Brown, A. R. Intro. to *African Systems of Kinship and Marriage*, p. 83.

baby was born, her mother had taken to 'popping round' two or three times a week.

'Mum helped when I was having the baby and I will say she was very good. The trouble is, she still wants to help. Every Wednesday she comes round to take my washing to the launderette. I'd do it myself, I don't really want her to, but she's always saying, "You mustn't do this, you mustn't do that. You've got the baby to look after." My husband says, "You tell her we don't need her coming round here all the time." But it's no good. Mum *must* come.'

Mrs Mann was pulled by conflicting loyalties. She said 'I like to see Mum of course,' but she was attached to her husband and understood his resentment when he complained 'She doesn't *mother* you, she *smothers* you.'

'If I don't see her nearly every day, she says, "Oh, I thought you was ill or something . . ." She doesn't actually interfere, but she's always making remarks. She says, "Baby seems to be crying a lot, doesn't he?" Or, "Oh, haven't you put him on the bottle yet?" My husband doesn't like it, I can tell you.'

Their tiny house has been 'condemned by the sanitary man' and is due for early demolition under a slum clearance scheme, so 'the Council has been round to see where we want to go'. Having talked it over 'we put our names down for a house at Greenleigh. My husband says it will cost more and he'll have the extra journey, but we can make our own life out there.'

As we shall see later in this book, some other families who move out to housing estates may be actuated by similar motives. As for the wives still living in Bethnal Green, they rarely make a sharp break with their mothers. They may sometimes bridle against Mum's authority, and even partly withdraw from her influence, but as long as the couple live near to the maternal home, she is usually seen fairly often; ninety out of the ninety-three wives in the general sample with mothers in the borough had seen them within the previous week.

If the wife's mother is living near, the couple somehow

have to adjust their lives to the fact that the wife is attached to her as well as to her husband. One course is for the husband to go his own way, spending a large part of his time away from his wife, not only during working hours, but at evenings and week-ends as well. Another is for him to be drawn into the maternal fold along with his wife. In the past, we would suspect, the second course was seldom followed, the pressures on the husband to exclude himself from the extended family, or be excluded, being too strong for most men to withstand. Today, if marriage is more often a partnership, then the couple is more likely, one would imagine, to be partners in the extended family as well.

The supposition seems to be borne out when the contacts of men and women with their respective mothers-in-law are compared. Of the people in the general sample who had a mother-in-law, seventy per cent of the husbands, against fifty-seven per cent of the wives, had seen them during the previous week. This shows the relative 'pull' of the two mothers – in Bethnal Green men are drawn into their wives' families to a greater extent than wives into their husbands'. After marriage, Mrs Sanderson told us, 'The sons usually go to their wives' families.'

Not all men behave in this way. If we consider in detail the twenty-six men in the marriage sample whose wives see their mother at least once a week, we find that although nineteen see their mothers-in-law once a week or more, the remaining seven see them less frequently. Judging by this crude yardstick, we could say that the first group have been drawn into the extended families to which their wives belong, and the second have not. We can label these two groups – the nineteen drawn into the extended family and the seven who remain outside it – as one of our informants, herself a Mum, distinguished her daughters' husbands. She called them the 'in-laws' and the 'outlaws'.

IN-LAWS AND OUTLAWS

The 'outlaws' told us little of their feelings about their mothers-in-law, and we found it difficult to explore a subject so obviously a source of embarrassment. One man insisted that he never saw his wife's mother: 'Do you hear that, Alice?' he shouted to his wife in the next room. 'How often do I see your mother? Ho, ho, that's good, ain't it? I never see her – never. I keep away from her.' Mrs Trimble said about her husband's contacts with her mother, 'He never goes round her place. When I go round he don't come. He only sees Mum when she comes round here – and that's not very often.'

Although, in these families, the husband seeks through 'mother-in-law avoidance'[1] to reduce the conflict between himself and his wife's mother, he may avoid conflict in the extended family only to aggravate it in his family of marriage. The wife is determined to keep in close touch with her mother. The husband resents Mum's power but, though he can avoid her direct influence, he cannot avoid the indirect effects of his wife's refusal to follow his example. He can keep away from his mother-in-law, but unless his wife keeps away from her too, the triangle may still be in tension.

What of the 'in-laws' who follow the more common Bethnal Green pattern? Some are drawn into Mum's empire reluctantly, not because they welcome her influence, but simply because they have to accept it as fact. An extreme example is the Mr Jones cited earlier. He dislikes his mother-in-law's interference, yet his life is tightly bound to hers just because he and his wife live in the same house with her.

Wherever the couple live close to the wife's mother, the husband may find he has hardly any choice but to accept his involvement in her extended family. He is sent round by his wife to borrow some bread when they run out on a Sunday. His wife is not at home when he gets back from work; knowing she will be 'round Mum's', off he goes to fetch her. Little Sandra, left at Mum's on a Saturday while her mother goes shopping, is waiting there to be collected by him. In

1. In some simpler societies this practice is adopted as a means of giving 'a stable, ordered form' to a social relationship which might otherwise produce conflict. Cf. Radcliffe-Brown, A. R. 'On Joking Relationships', p. 92.

countless ways, if his wife's life is focused on her mother, then so too is his.

The majority of the 'in-laws' accept their role with good grace. As far as we could judge, most men are reconciled to their mother-in-law, and their mother-in-law to them. Some actually enjoy her company and speak of her with obvious warmth, like Mr Wilkins, who said, 'People complain about their mothers-in-law, but my wife's mother is one of the best in the world.'

COURTING THE MOTHER-IN-LAW

It is clear that the mutual adjustment of the husband to his wife's family, and particularly to his mother-in-law, is a crucial matter. If husband and mother-in-law do not get on, the marriage will be stormy, the wife pulled this way and that by competing loyalties. This helps to explain why the very first visit of a man to his future bride's family is thought more of an event than that of the girl to his family. 'Any mother wants to have a look at her daughter's young man,' as one woman said. 'She wants to see the goods laid out on the table.' 'It was like Judge and Jury,' said Mr Little about the first meeting with his mother-in-law.

'I came from Scanlon Street,' he went on. 'That used to be considered a rough part. It seems silly now, but her turning was a little bit above mine socially. It must have been six months or a year before I went round the wife's house to meet them. I remember that all right, with her mother's eyes on me all the time.'

This first formal visit is less of an ordeal for the man who already has family connexions with his future wife. Five out of the forty-five men in the marriage sample were first introduced to their wife by her brother, sister, or other relative, and a further eight couples actually grew up together in the same street. 'We lived here when we were children,' said Mrs Sykes, 'that's how we met. Our families knew each other. My mother knew his mother when they was girls – even before *they* were married. The families grew up together.'

Where the families know each other as well as this, the prospective son-in-law is half way into the wife's family before he even starts courting. Whether this is so or not, during the engagement the couple usually foreshadow the future by spending more time at the wife's home. We were able to observe one of these regular visits, for we happened to arrive for the interview when the young man was in attendance at his fiancée's home. Mum and Dad – she a middle-aged, stout, friendly-faced woman; he, though friendly, more cautious, a tough, laconic docker – were sitting in the place of honour by the fireside in the only two chairs with arms. A ten-year-old daughter and her elder sister, married and nursing a baby on her lap, were watching the television, while the latter's husband, just home from work, sat at the table eating his tea (a chop, boiled potatoes, and peas) and her brother George, twenty-three and still single, rushed about, washing in the kitchen, combing his hair and fixing his tie in front of the mirror above the fireplace, preparatory to 'going out with the boys'. By the wall near the door sat nineteen-year-old Jean and her boy Freddie, holding hands, looking at the television when they took their eyes off each other, and giggling occasionally at the rigmarole of extraordinary questions.

If he does his courting in this fashion, sitting on his future mother-in-law's chairs, watching her television, drinking her cups of tea, if he gets to know his bride's close relatives intimately, then his adjustment to them and theirs to him is a very gradual one, and if all goes well he becomes accepted almost as a member of the family, even before he marries. He rehearses while a suitor his future role of son-in-law as well as husband. The latent tensions may remain, but mother, daughter, and husband will learn by process of trial and error to get on together in the small things without falling out over the big.

Whether mother and son-in-law are reconciled to each other before or after the wedding, the reconciliation is, as we have seen, usually achieved. After marriage, the son-in-law is frequently so absorbed into the extended family that it becomes as much the setting for his life as for his wife's. Mr Robbins is one of the eleven men in the marriage sample who sees his mother-in-law at least once a day:

'I've got my drinking friends,' he said, 'that's my brothers-in-law mostly.[1] We're a proper mixing family. I see the wife's mother at least once every day and most of her sisters and my brothers-in-law too. All the brothers-in-law go out together – mix in the same company, use the same pubs, have the same activities, follow the same sports. At the week-ends we all take our wives along when we can, so it's a real family gathering round the pub – us two and the wife's sisters and all their husbands and the wife's mother and father. Annie's eldest girl – she's thirteen – she usually gives eye to our two and comes up and tells us if they wake up.'

Mr Banton said he sees his wife's parents 'mostly every day':

'The boy goes over the wife's mother's to play every day – he's used to it because her mother always used to look after him when the wife worked. I go over and collect him on the way back from work and I nearly always go indoors and have a cup of tea.'

He also goes swimming at the York Hall Baths in the summer with Albie, his wife's unmarried brother: 'Albie's his mate,' Mrs Banton told us. And, although Mr Banton calls to see his own parents regularly every Sunday morning, the week-ends are otherwise mainly spent with his in-laws – 'We always see her family at the week-ends.'

Others do the same. It is common for at least part of the week-end to be spent round at Mum's.

'My husband and I go with the kiddies round to my Mum's nearly every Sunday evening. It's not a regular thing, but we usually find ourselves up there.'

'Every Saturday night we take Alan (their four-year-old son) round and all watch the T.V. at Mum's.'

'We go round to Mum's every Friday and Saturday and we play cards or watch the tellie. My sisters and their husbands always go round there too.'

1. Mr Robbins is here referring to his wife's sisters' husbands as his 'brothers-in-law'.

It is the same at Christmas, at birthday parties, at all the family gatherings except the funerals or weddings to which a wider circle of kin are invited. The common pattern – in extended families where the sons-in-law are 'in-laws' rather than 'outlaws' – is for the daughters and their husbands to go round to Mum's for the occasion. When Mrs Cole was asked who would be going to her mother's birthday party on the following Saturday, she said her sisters and their husbands, and the boy-friend of her remaining unmarried sister Lucy, but not her married brothers.

'These same people always go,' she said. 'It's always the same mob. They're our closest friends – our closest family. It'll be Lucy's 21st birthday soon and all the same mob will go to that as well.'

For family gatherings the operative family is the wife's, and it is her parental home, not her husband's, that the couple visit. Mum's is the centre for sons-in-law as well as daughters. The husband joins his wife's family as a kind of associate member. His wife remains a full member, owing to his relatives little of the allegiance he owes to hers.

HUSBANDS ARE ALSO SONS

But however fully he enters his wife's family, the husband does not resign from his own. The men are not drawn right out of their own families into their wives'; they tend to see more of their wives' kin, it is true, but they keep in closer touch with both families than their wives. Two-thirds of the men in the general sample with mothers alive had seen them in the previous week, nearly one third in the previous day. Husbands in the marriage sample, though they saw their mothers-in-law about three times a week on average, still saw their own mothers just over twice a week.

In a district in which husbands and wives so often have both parents near, these contacts might perhaps be chance meetings in the street. But this is not so. In the interviews with the marriage sample we were struck time and again by the regularity with which men kept in touch with their parents, usually calling at the same time each week. 'I go

73

down on my own to see the old lady every Thursday regular.'
'He goes round there every Friday evening; I don't see her
more than three times a year myself.' 'I go round every
Sunday regular, even if I've seen them in the week already,'
said Mr Banton, a lorry-driver. 'On my job I'm often passing that way; if I do, I just look in to see them then. When
I go on Sunday I usually take the two youngsters round with
me while the wife gets the dinner.'

Although some men, when parents live in the East End,
are accompanied by their wives on these visits, it is com-
moner for the men to go alone or just with their children.
Although fathers are seen as often as mothers, the regular
visit to the parents seems to be chiefly inspired by a sense
of duty to the mother. We were often told 'I go to see her'
or 'my mother', rather than 'them' or 'my parents'. 'I've
got a great affection for my mother,' said one man. 'I more
or less consider it my duty to see her once a week and give
her a few bob and see she's all right.' 'I make it my business
to call round to see my mother every Sunday,' said Mr Wilkins. 'I never miss a week.' Another husband suggested the
triumph of duty over inclination when he said, 'I usually
go round on a Sunday morning. You can't ignore them –
they only live round the corner.' This feeling of obligation
was recognized by the wives, who expected their husbands
to keep up their regular weekly visits. 'He goes round to see
her regular,' said one woman. 'Naturally, she's his mother,
isn't she?' Marriage apart, the mother-son bond is recognized in Bethnal Green as being secondary only to that between mother and daughter.

For one reason or another, the husband's mother may
sometimes play a fuller part in the life of the family of marriage. The couple and their children may be drawn to the
husband's family of origin rather than the wife's, so that the
mother is as much a key person in her son's family as in her
daughter's. This may happen because the wife has quarrelled
with her mother. Or the husband's mother may have no
daughters while the wife's mother has a number, so that the
husband feels strongly that he and his family should stay

74

1. mom/daughter
2. mom/son
3. husband/wife

close to her, and his wife that it is proper to depart from the usual pattern, particularly if her mother-in-law is a widow. But it appeared from our small marriage sample that the most common reason was that her own mother was dead, with no close women relatives to take her place.

When Mr Plant, for instance, met his bride in Carlisle during the war she was an orphan, so she came down to Bethnal Green after the wedding and lived with his parents until he was demobbed. Now the couple usually go down to his parents' home at the week-ends with the children, and, as Mr Plant put it, 'sometimes in the week the wife takes the kiddies down there alone. I pop down every day.' 'She couldn't be better if she was my own mother,' said Mrs Brown about her mother-in-law; her own mother died when she was ten and she had no sisters.

'Being so long without a mother of my own,' she went on, 'I suppose I took to her from the beginning. When I was younger – a teenager - I used to envy the other girls who had mothers. Mum – she's always been "Mum" to me – Mum's always been helpful; she's always looked upon me as a daughter. Had I had a mother of my own I expect I'd have stuck to her like anyone would, but as it was I was more than willing to accept someone who was willing to accept me.'

This chapter has been concerned for the most part with the more common constellation when the wife's mother is the mistress of her family. Then, we have seen, the husband is usually drawn into his mother-in-law's sphere and comes to accept the new order of his life, relations often becoming smoother when the couple convert the mother-in-law into a grandmother. However it is done, the typical conflict between the man and the older woman is, by means of a compromise, usually reduced or at least held in check, and the dual loyalties of the two principal actors reconciled.

5

THE KINSHIP NETWORK

IN this chapter we shall again consider the influence of the mother, this time not directly upon her daughter and son-in-law but upon their relationships with her other children and their other kin. To do this we have to depart from the approach we have adopted so far. Up to now we have been fixing our gaze on the present circumstances of people quite deliberately chosen at roughly the same stage of their lives. They were all married, they were all fairly young, they all had dependent children. This was all very well when we were talking about the couples themselves, even about the couples and their parents. But such a simplified, indeed static, approach will not do any longer.

The reason is that, although the couples are all at roughly the same stage of their lives, their parents are not. Dead people could not get into the sample, but people with dead parents could, and did. We have mentioned death before – in the last chapter, for instance, where we said that some wives whose own mothers were dead drew upon the support of their mothers-in-law instead. But we have done so in passing, believing it better to proceed one step at a time. Now we have to consider people with dead parents separately from people whose parents are alive, and to take into account the passage of time. We are driven to do this by the evident fact that the relations with siblings[1] (of the seventy-eight of the ninety men and women in the marriage sample who had them) are so dependent on the existence of their parents. We have to try and view the kinship system more as a dynamic process than we have done so far.

1. Siblings are children of the same parents, i.e. brothers and sisters. An Anglo-Saxon term which meant 'relatives', it has now been adopted by anthropologists and others, who use it in this more limited sense. We propose to follow the same practice.

We begin with the people whose parents, and especially their mothers, are alive. In the relations of brothers and sisters to each other the mother makes her influence felt throughout. Her daughters, at least those who have continued to live locally, are members of the same extended family. Her other daughters who live further away, together with her sons, usually make regular visits to see her. The siblings see a good deal of each other because they all see a good deal of Mum. Her daughters see her more than her sons, and as a result one would expect that the sisters see more of each other than brothers see of sisters or of each other. Table 8, which applies to all siblings wherever they live, shows that this is so.

TABLE 8: Contacts of Men and Women with their Siblings

(General sample)

	Brothers		Sisters	
	Number of brothers	Percentage of brothers seen in previous week	Number of sisters	Percentage of sisters seen in previous week
Men	755	27%	769	35%
Women	701	42%	750	52%

Both sons and daughters see their mother (and each other) at her home more than anywhere else. 'I generally see my brothers and sisters round at Mum's,' said Mrs Power. 'There's always one or other of my sisters round there. If anyone wants to know what's going on, they always go round to Mum's.' 'As for my brothers and sisters,' Mr Banton told us, 'I don't go knocking at their doors or anything like that. If I see them it's either when I'm calling on Mum or else up the Bethnal Green Road.' 'I see my sister Edna every day,' said Mrs Madge, who lives with her parents. 'She comes round to have dinner with Mum every day. She's got nerves, and she doesn't like to be on her own all day.'

Even when the mother's home is not the siblings' meeting place, she may still be the main link between them. Mrs Little's mother, an invalid, lives with another of her daughters at Epsom. This daughter, according to Mrs Little, 'comes up twice a week regular from Epsom to tell me how mother is'.

THE MOTHER'S MEMORY

We now move on to see what happens when the mother dies. The first and most obvious effect is that, since her children no longer visit her home, they see less of each other. Of the 162 married, widowed, and divorced women in the general sample with their mothers alive, 35 per cent had seen a sister in the previous day, against 16 per cent of the 242 whose mothers were dead. 'It all broke up when Mum died,' said one woman. 'There's been no head of the family – no organization. We just take it into our head to go and see one another.' 'We used to spend Christmas together until the old lady died,' another informant told us, 'and then we all separated.' One man, a dustman, said of his wife's relatives: 'We don't see much of them since Mum died – Mum's used to be the central depot in this family.'

But in a sense the mother does not die; her memory remains alive. Mrs Ruck produced with pride a picture not of her mother but of the tombstone: the words TOO WELL LOVED TO BE FORGOTTEN were picked out in black on the granite. As another woman tenderly passed over her mother's photograph, she said: 'Mum and I was like sisters. Why do they argue with their mothers? I hear them on the landings. I tell them I don't see it. They'll regret it.'

Even after her death, the mother who lives on in this way is sometimes the means of bringing the siblings together. If they are not able to share her company, they can at least share her memory. 'Not a week goes by,' said Mr Aves, 'but one of us goes down to Manor Park to put flowers on mother's grave.' Mr Glass's family go so far as to meet every year on the anniversary of the dead mother's birthday:

'We take it in turns to be host. All my brothers and sisters are musical and sing. This year the do was here. We had lots to eat in the front room and singing and fooling around.'

Even without such formal gatherings the mother's influence may extend beyond the grave.

'When my mother was alive she carried on my insurance policy for me. Now that she's dead, the collector still calls at her place every month. My sister Sarah took the place over when Mum died and she's gone on paying the collector for me. That's why I see her every fortnight – I call round to give her my insurance.'

It would be going too far to say that the siblings are only held together by the mother's memory. They have an organization to some extent autonomous. This is shown by the convention that one of the sisters or one of the brothers, usually the eldest, acts as 'head' of the family in the absence of the parents, incidentally a convention supported by the practice of naming the eldest sons and daughters after their parents.

This sometimes happened long before the mother died. The eldest daughter, in particular, often had to act as a 'little mother' to her younger siblings, while her mother was out at work or ill. 'My family was costers,' said one woman. 'I was the oldest and had to stay at home and look after the others while Mum was in the street.' If the family was a large one the mother might have been quite unable to manage without the help of a daughter – 'I was the oldest of thirteen and looked after most of them to help my mother out.'

The pattern of childhood may be repeated in later life: Mr Aves told us, 'My father was killed in the First World War. I was the eldest one of the family – and I was only eleven at the time. My mother had to work really hard to bring us up. That's one reason why I try to keep the family together now that she's gone. They all look on me as the head of the family and I've more or less made it my job to keep them together.' The responsibility assumed during the mother's lifetime continues after her death, and to 'keep the family together' is to keep faith with her.

Mr Aves is an eldest brother who was in a special position of authority because he had taken over some of the father's functions in childhood. It is apparently more common in large families for the others to turn to the eldest sister after the mother's death. 'Edie mothers Jessie and me,' said one woman about her eldest sister. 'We were the two who were still at home with her when Mum died during the war. All the sisters go round to Edie's.'

Mrs Firth is herself an eldest sister who has maintained a close organization. She and her younger sister were both married before their mother died and spent a good deal of their time at her home. The only brother, who is still single, moved in to live with Mrs Firth after the mother's death, and still does so. 'When mother died,' Mrs Firth said, 'I told him he could come and live with us.' 'My sister comes round here to dinner every day,' she added. 'We're always together. We haven't no parents and I think that brings you closer together. When we go out, there's always the six of us, my husband and me, my sister and her husband, and my brother and his girl friend – and the children of course. If we have a party it's always the same six.' Mrs Firth runs a family credit club and in addition she collects money from the others for Christmas: 'We put away 2s. 6d. a week each all through the year. Then we lay that money out at Christmas to see we have a good time. We start planning about a fortnight before Christmas how we're going to spend the money.'

As far as we could judge, Mrs Firth and her sister were on the friendliest terms. But it seems that the eldest sibling, having some of the authority of the parents, is sometimes regarded with a certain awe. 'I like Milly all right,' one woman said, 'but I always remember that she's the eldest. I feel she's a bit hard inside.' In a large family, the eldest sibling may be as much as twenty years older than the youngest, and in families like these there seems to be a special tie with the 'nearest sibling'. 'I see most of Alan,' said Mr Marsh. 'He's the nearest to me. By the time I started school all the other brothers were courting and so there wasn't much in common.' Mrs Gould felt especially close to her 'nearest' sister, Joy, and recalled the times they had had together as children. 'Oh, you should see how we were at home. Joy and me had a curtain for a top sheet. I used to say "Aren't we smart, Joy?" and she would say "Them holes is for the bugs to crawl through." Oh, she's a scream.'

So the siblings usually keep in touch with each other after the mother's death. If they live at a distance from each other and do not meet often, they still communicate with each other. They send Christmas and birthday cards, and keep the family news flowing.[1] The people we interviewed on the housing estate at Greenleigh – to anticipate a later part of the book – were able to tell us something about the means by which this was done. They were, for the most part, couples who had left their relatives behind them when they left Bethnal Green: if their parents were still alive, then they visited them and the mother was again the link with other siblings. If their parents were dead, then a sibling, often the eldest sister, acted post office. Mr Windle said: 'Rene (the eldest sister) keeps us all closely knitted. We all look towards her and she sees that we're all right. She passes on all the gen from the others.'

UNMARRIED BROTHERS AND SISTERS

Over half of all the unmarried people in the general sample (82 out of 137) were living with their parents. One would imagine that when parents die the single men and women would then be more on their own than their married brothers and their married sisters who are at this time beginning to establish new extended families in replacement of those they have lost. In fact, what often happens is that one of the other siblings, a sister usually, takes over the responsibility for any single sibling formerly in the mother's care.

The substitute mother may be unmarried herself. 'My

1. Another study of family behaviour, in the East Coast floods of 1953, noted the speed with which people flooded-out of homes on Canvey Island informed their relatives in East London. See Young, M. 'The Role of the Extended Family in a Disaster'.

younger brother, Freddie, and me were still living at home when Mum died,' one woman told us. 'We stayed on there and I looked after him. We've always been very close.' Or she may already be married like Mrs Firth and Mrs James, who both have an unmarried brother living with them. Certainly many of the single adults of all ages not with parents are living with a single or married sibling, as Table 9 shows.

TABLE 9: Residence of Single People not
Living with Parents

(General sample – 55 single adults not living with parents)

	Men	Women
Living with single or married siblings	16	11
Living with other relatives	2	3
Not living with relatives	10	23
TOTAL	28	27

Siblings provide the main support and sisters more than brothers, a large majority of the single people living with married siblings being with sisters.

This attachment of a single sibling to the family of a married sister may, if he or she never marries, continue right through life. We met, in the intensive interviews, two extended families in which the Mum's single sister was an additional member: one was Mrs Warner's Aunt Ada who 'lives round the corner near Mum. She's always round Mum's in the daytime and she's often round here as well. She and Mum take turns to give eye to the children for us. Oh, she's a great favourite, Aunt Ada is.'

Our main subjects are married couples with young children. We have so far been describing their relations with their families of origin, and have shown that when brothers and sisters are introduced, it does, if anything, further enhance the importance of the mother whose role we considered from various angles in previous chapters. We now move outwards again to review, very briefly, the place of other relatives, that is the people to whom the couples are linked by their parents.

Naturally enough, these do not play so large a part as siblings. Husbands and wives saw their siblings on average five times more frequently than they saw their uncles and aunts, for example. But these more distant kin still need to be mentioned to make our account anything like complete.

THE WIDER NETWORK

The review needs only to be brief because in a sense there is nothing basically new to say. The description we have given of the families of origin of wife and husband applies to the families of origin of their parents as well. The difference is merely that the parents' families of origin are at another stage of life. Whereas some of the husbands and wives no longer have parents, nearly all the parents' parents are dead and this influences *their* relations with *their* siblings as much as it does those of our couples with theirs.

The same process of change in family structure can be viewed again through the eyes of our informants, but this time they are speaking of the ascendant generations instead of their own. When they were children, some of them frequently saw their uncles and aunts, who were then still attached to living parents. Having grandparents, they were also more likely to have uncles and aunts in their lives. One of our older husbands, who had married children himself, said of his own childhood when his grandmother was still alive –

'When I was a boy I used to see a lot of my uncles and aunts and cousins. When you grow up you drop off seeing them. You keep up with your parents and your brothers and sisters though – you do that even after you get married. Now my parents are dead, I see my children and grandchildren most of all.'

When the grandparents died, that in itself weakened the ties between uncles and aunts, although one of them might (as we have seen before in another context) maintain the ties by taking over some of the grandparents' functions.

'Until my grandmother's death all the aunts and uncles, with their children, met at her house for her birthday and Christmas. They all come to see my mother now as the eldest sister on one of the holidays or at Christmas.'

In this way or another the uncles and aunts belonging to a particular family of origin usually continued to see at least something of each other. From the point of view of our informants, what mattered most was whether their own parents were alive If they were, they then acted as intermediaries with their siblings, that is with our informants' uncles and aunts. If they were dead, the connexion with the uncles and aunts was also lost. When your mother dies, said Mrs Firth, 'you lose contact with your uncles and aunts.' When a particular uncle or aunt died, a link with a set of relatives was lost, just as it was when the parents died. 'You lose track of your cousins', said Mrs Jeffreys, 'once your aunts have gone.'

The distinction we have made between the families of origin of the husbands and wives and the families of origin of their parents was one that our informants made on ritual occasions. The ordinary *rites de passage* are observed in Bethnal Green, as elsewhere, by appropriate ceremonials for engagements, weddings, christenings, and funerals. People come together at these times to give support to a relative at a turning point in his life, to express their solidarity, and to reinforce the attachment they feel to each other and to the family. The rituals are family gatherings, but not always for the same families. At christenings, for instance, the husbands and wives invite only parents and siblings. The party Mrs Robbins had for the christening of her youngest child was not unusual.

'My parents and his came and my sisters and their husbands and his brothers and sisters and their husbands and wives. We had a little tea in the afternoon and then a few drinks later on. Nothing strenuous, though. It was all family, except that Jack brought one of his mates along because he plays the piano.'

The fact that christenings are an affair for siblings is shown by the choice of godparents for the children. Nearly two thirds of the godparents (for the children of the forty-five couples) were siblings of either husband or wife, usually one from each side. 'We had one from each side every time,' said Mrs Power, 'either one of my sisters and one of his brothers or the other way round.'

Weddings are bigger events. Each couple in the marriage sample had an average of twenty-one adult relatives at their wedding, as compared with only seven at the christening of their youngest child. This was because invitations were usually extended to the families of origin of the parents as well as to those of the bride and bridegroom. The same goes for funerals. The proper thing is for the dead person's siblings (and his spouses's siblings) to attend, as well as his descendants. Thus when Mrs Sanderson's mother died, the maternal uncles and aunts and the two paternal uncles came to the funeral, together with their spouses and one or two of the children of each of them. It is apparently customary for at least one of the adult children of each of the uncles and aunts to accompany them, but not young children, who are by convention excluded. When Mrs Prince's maternal aunt was buried, Mrs Prince went with her mother.

'Mum sent the money to pay my fare up to Ada's funeral. She wanted me to go with her as the eldest child to be there for the family.'

For this occasion the children take pains to find their uncles and aunts even if they have lost touch almost completely. Mr Merton said that:

'When Dad died we went to Wembley to the road where we thought one of his brothers lived, and gave the letter with the news of the death to someone who knew him by name. It got to him in the end.'

Consequently, relatives may be at the funeral who are hardly seen at any other time. 'I haven't seen any of my uncles and aunts for ages,' said one woman. 'The last time was after my father died when they came down to the funeral to pay their respects '

The attenders at funerals and weddings are in the ordinary way the widest span of relatives with whom contact is maintained. A person's kinship network extends no farther than to his grandparents and their descendants. Since descent is not usually traced farther back than this, there cannot be a wide spread of recognized relatives of the same generation. If the effective common ancestor is not more than two generations away, then people cannot normally trace relationships to collaterals beyond first cousins. It is only (as we shall mention in a moment) when they are living very near to more remote relatives, such as second cousins and great-uncles, that they enter into their lives; and only then that the effective common ancestor becomes a great-grandparent rather than a grandparent.

PROXIMITY OF RELATIVES

Who is in a person's kinship network, and the character of the relationships within it, depend primarily upon the stage of life reached by himself and by his relatives. That is the gist of what we have been saying so far in this chapter. But we cannot leave the subject without mentioning again the influence of proximity which interacts continuously with family structure. Geography is an influence as well as genealogy.

Leaving out parents, the forty-five couples in the marriage sample taken together had between them 1,691 relatives within the degrees shown in Table 10. Of these, 578, or 34 per cent, lived in the borough and a further 324, or 19 per cent, in an adjacent borough. For each couple, the average number of relatives living in Bethnal Green was thirteen and all but four couples had some relatives in the borough.

Couples in Bethnal Green who have not only their parents in the district, but other relatives also, are liable to see them merely because they live in the same territory.

'One of my mother's sisters lives just up the street. We don't visit, but we bang into each other nearly every day.'

TABLE 10: Numbers of Relatives other than Parents Living in Bethnal Green

(Marriage sample – 45 couples with 1,691 relatives)

	Number of relatives, excluding parents, in Bethnal Green					
	None	1–4	5–9	10–19	20–29	30 and over
Number of couples	4	8	12	9	7	5

Relatives include siblings, siblings' spouses, uncles and aunts, nephews and nieces, and grandparents, but not cousins or more remote kin.

'My aunts and uncles all live round here so I often see them. I usually stop for a chin-wag.'

'I see my aunt up the market sometimes and tell her how Mum's getting on.'

'I've got a lot of cousins and second cousins living round Hanley Street, and I'm always seeing them round the Green.'

The relatives in Table 10 are those of the *couples*; in other words, from the viewpoint of any individual husband (or wife) they include his 'in-laws' as well as his 'own' relatives. Everyone's relatives are augmented by marriage, and one explanation for the number of relatives living nearby is that a large proportion of marriages in Bethnal Green are between local people, both of whom may have kindred in the vicinity: 64 per cent of the married people in the general sample had both themselves been born in the locality (in Bethnal Green or in an adjacent borough), and had married spouses born within it.

In this chapter we have, to conclude, been considering other relatives beside parents. The analysis has been in two parts. We began with the siblings belonging to our informants' families of origin. Sometimes these are attached to an extended family consisting of the mother, her daughters (and to a lesser extent her sons), and the daughters' husbands and children. But whether or not they are, contact is usually maintained between siblings as long as the mother is alive, and is not usually severed even after the mother is dead. In the second part we briefly discussed the other relatives in the kinship network. They are for the most part members of the families of origin of the parents, or the spouses and children of the uncles and aunts. Unless they happen to live nearby, more remote relatives than these are not usually recognized.

We have in this and the previous chapters, briefly described some of the chief relationships of the local kinship system. Before we move on to Greenleigh, it only remains to consider the interaction of the family and certain other institutions which are also of great importance in the life of Bethnal Green.

6

THE FAMILY IN THE ECONOMY

WE suggested in an earlier chapter that since most married women have the same work to do, in caring for child and home, their job reinforces their kinship and makes the mother-daughter tie pre-eminent. We must now inquire whether the men of the family are held together likewise. Do son and father follow the same occupation or not? Is the brotherhood of work a figure of speech or a statement of fact? The economic structure is one thing, kinship another. How, if at all, do they affect one another? To answer this question we must digress for a moment to describe the chief features of the local economy.

You do not have to live in Bethnal Green, you only have to take a bus down the main street, to notice that this is a place of many industries. You pass tailors' workshops, furniture makers, Kearley & Tonge's food warehouse, and near to Allen & Hanbury's big factory. The borough has by itself a more diversified economy than some countries. But the borough has no frontiers: it belongs to the economy which stretches down both banks of the Thames. At its heart is the largest port in the world, which lines the river for nearly twenty miles from London Bridge to Tilbury, and supports on every side a web of interconnected industries – ship-repairers and ship-suppliers, docks and lighterage, stores and depots, railways and motor transport, and the thousands of manufacturers, warehousemen, and merchants who process and pass tea and coffee, palm oil and wool, spices and hides, meat and wheat, from half the world on into the metropolis and the interior.

The port has added to diversity by giving entry not only to economy. Because the East End is a port, and near to the Continent, it is the place where for centuries foreigners have landed to escape from war and persecution in Europe. Long before the Luftwaffe set the docks and houses ablaze and accelerated the migration to the suburbs, more beneficent invasions contributed to the rich variety of East End life. The Huguenots, fleeing from the religious persecution in France, especially after the Edict of Nantes was revoked in 1685, can stand as the founders of Bethnal Green as an industrial centre. Prevented from settling in the City by the restrictions of the guilds, they established their silk looms and other trades in Spitalfields and Bethnal Green. Today there are no longer even the few hand-loom weavers who survived until 1939 and the last Huguenot silk firm closed its lofty weaving rooms in 1955. The furniture-making which started as an offshoot of the silk upholstery trade has supplanted its parent and although it too has been declining for many years, it is still one of the staple industries. Charles Booth's description at the end of the last century is still apposite. 'Of the Bethnal Green trade,' he says, 'Gossett Street . . . may be considered the centre, and in the immediate neighbourhood of this street the atmosphere of the trade pervades the whole area . . . there are no warehouses; even large workshops are few and far between, and the most conspicuous signs of the chief crafts of the district are the timber-yards and the saw-mills. But in many of the houses, and in nearly every workshop, furniture is being made . . . chairmakers, cabinet makers, turners, and carvers abound. It is the region of small makers.'[1]

Other industries have been less successful in withstanding the competition of mechanized production, despite the advantage of proximity to the London market for consumer goods. Boot and shoe making is not as important as it used to be, nor is the tailoring[2] which the Jewish refugees promoted and sustained for many years after they escaped from the ghettoes of Eastern Europe. Yet small-scale industry struggles on in sawmills, caster-making, locks, hinges, dowels, glass, organ-building, and in all the other little trades of the

1. Booth, C. op. cit. p. 161.
2. So vividly described in its early days by Beatrice Webb. See Potter, B. 'The Jewish Community'.

district. There are, as well as the large breweries, Mann's and Truman's, the railways, and the few bigger factories, still hundreds of small masters employing a few men in one of the residential houses which have been as much the home of Bethnal Green industry as of its people. One of the most characteristic sights of the streets is a pile of legs, shelves, and chairs being trundled on a hand-cart from one sub-contractor to another. The mentality of the master-craftsman which was one of the outstanding marks of the working class in the nineteenth century still survives too. The master-craftsman produced the sweat-shops – Booth spoke of 'the multiplication of small masters that was the tap-root of sweating' – and also an attitude of outspoken independence and a range of trades, customs, and personality which has added to the variety of local society as much as it has detracted from its prosperity.[1]

As the old industries have declined, the economy of Bethnal Green has merged ever more closely into the wider economy of the East End. Even in 1921, 58 per cent of the working population of the borough worked outside it and the proportion had increased to 68 per cent by 1951. The majority of those who worked outside the borough did not, however, have far to travel – two-thirds of them working in one of the adjoining boroughs of Stepney, Shoreditch, Poplar, or Hackney, or in the nearby City of London.[2]

This diversified economy in, and even more beyond, the borough is a boon to the family. When dependent on one or a few industries, the family is as vulnerable as the district. Their economic foundation is treacherous. When the coal, steel, and other heavy industries of areas like South Wales were hit by the pre-war depression, men had to desert their native hearth in search of work, and when they left home they had to leave many of their relatives behind. East London is less vulnerable because it has many industries to lean on, and while it cannot avoid being harmed by a general

1. Cf. Munby, D. L. *Industry and Planning in Stepney*, p. 168.
2. *Census*, 1951. *England and Wales. Report on Usual Residence and Workplace*, Table 5, pp. 128–9.

contraction in trade, particularly in overseas trade, at least there is a good chance that even then some of its industries will be able to save themselves from the general decline. When people lose their jobs in one employment they can usually get jobs elsewhere within daily travelling distance and, if that happens, they do not have to leave their homes.

Economic variety yields advantage even when times are good. In the one-industry town or village the son must follow his father's occupation because there is no other: unless he is to leave home, the son of miner or farm-worker must become a miner or a farm-worker too. Which is one reason that those with no love for coal or land do go off to the city, even when mining or agriculture are themselves prosperous and short of labour. By contrast, East London offers such bountiful choice that sons and daughters can usually take the job of their liking without leaving home. The city which does so much to create change, by holding up a thousand different models of behaviour, compensates in this way for the vicissitudes which it fosters. Some of those evacuated in the war remarked on its merit. Mrs Glass was delighted with the friendliness of the small Lancashire town where she stayed with her husband, yet wanted to come back all the same.

'It wouldn't do to stay there. In London if he has words with the boss or doesn't like anything, he can walk out and get into another firm. In Lancashire there was only one firm in his trade.'

In this way economic variety helps to maintain family stability; children can live in the same place as their parents without following the same career. But in another way, economic variety may weaken family solidarity on the man's side. In such a place as this, sons have many different examples before them. Their father's job is only one of many. They can, if they wish, get other jobs in other industries, and when they do, their interests, attitudes, and associates are not the same as their fathers'. In Bethnal Green we would not expect the father-son tie to be stressed by importing into the family the solidarity of work, as it would probably be in any place with a narrow industrial base.

A WORKING-CLASS QUARTER

Although the jobs of East London are almost endless in their variety, they have one affinity: they are mostly manual work. Since those so engaged are usually thought of (if we exclude such as surgeons, dentists, and sculptors) as belonging to the 'working class', the whole of East London is a vast one-class quarter. The social classes of Bethnal Green, which is like the other local boroughs, are compared in Table 11 with the Census figures for Great Britain.

TABLE 11: Social Class of Occupied Men

	Bethnal Green General Sample 1955	Great Britain Census 1951
Higher professional	1%	3%
Lower professional	5%	15%
Clerical	12%	8%
Skilled manual	49%	45%
Semi-skilled manual	11%	16%
Unskilled manual	22%	13%
TOTAL	100%	100%

Here, as elsewhere in this book, we use the Registrar-General's classification of social classes. Occupations are assigned to one or other class in *Classification of Occupations*, 1950. 'Higher professional' coincides with the Registrar-General's Class I; 'Lower professional' with his Class II; 'Clerical' and 'Skilled manual' with Class III; 'Semi-skilled manual' with Class IV; and 'Unskilled manual' with Class V. The source for the data for Great Britain is the *1 per cent Sample Tables, Census*, 1951.

The overwhelming majority of Bethnal Green men are manual workers, with a particularly high proportion of unskilled people. It is worth noting, too, that the professional classes are not like those elsewhere. The local government officers, teachers, doctors, welfare workers, and managers of the borough do not, on the whole, live within its borders. They travel in to their work every morning from outside.

More than half of the 'white-collar' people in our general sample actually living in Bethnal Green were shopkeepers and publicans, in many ways more akin to the working-class people they serve than to the professional men and administrators with whom they are classified. The tone of the district is set by the working class.

Since they have similar jobs, the people also have much in common. They have the same formal education. They usually reach their maximum earnings at the age of twenty-one and stay at that level, unless all wages advance, for the rest of their lives. Though wages may vary from £8 to £20 a week, they are nearly all paid by the hour. They are no more secure than other hourly-paid employees, liable to be dismissed without notice and deprived of pay during sickness, and, to counter insecurity, they have built the same trade union and political organizations. Every constituency in East London returns a Labour member to Parliament and every council is controlled by the Labour Party, Bethnal Green regularly electing a complete slate of Labour councillors almost as a matter of course. The people share their politics; they speak the same language with the same accents; they work with their hands; they have, in short, the same kind of life. These deep-lying bonds between members of a class are also bonds between members of the family.

SPEAKING TO THE GUV'NOR

Since relatives often have the same kind of work, they can sometimes help each other to get jobs. They do this in the same way as they get houses for each other – by putting in a good word in the right quarter – and reputation counts for one as much as for the other. A mother with a record of always being prompt with the rent has a good chance of getting a house for a daughter; a father with a record of being a good workman has a good chance of getting a job for his son, or indeed for any other relative he may recommend. Mr Meadows's father, for instance, worked for a

94

large motor transport undertaking for twenty-five years until he retired, and in all that time 'he never bothered and he never complained'. When Mr Meadows lost his own job as a furniture craftsman in a firm no longer able to compete with mass production, his father suggested he try transport.

'He recommended me to go for it and said it was a good job if you're prepared to work hard. I went to see the Personnel Officer at Head Office and he said "nothing doing". I said then I'd come because my father asked me to call. He said "Oh, yes. Who's that, your father?" and I said "Mr Meadows." He said "Oh yes, I know Mr Meadows. He used to work here, didn't he? Hang on a minute." He went out and in a few minutes he came back and said, "Yes, Meadows, we can fix you up."'

This kind of influence, though it still matters, is, we gathered, less important than it was before the war when local unemployment was, if not as high as in some parts of the country, certainly high enough to be felt or feared in almost every family. The task for a man was to get a job, almost any job, and to hold it against competition. If he was out of work, and a relative could persuade an employer to take him on, it was indeed a good turn. That was in a buyer's market. Since the war the whole situation has been reversed and for the time being most people have a wide choice of jobs. Employers have been searching for workers and, without having to be persuaded by a relative, some of them would hire almost anyone. In this new situation the kindred are less important as references than as a kind of informal labour exchange. People get news all the time from their relatives about the jobs with better pay, better conditions, or more overtime, and their comparisons may induce men to change. 'I got my present job as a lorry driver through my brother-in-law,' said Mr Little. 'At that time I used to work for Blundells and he came down there and saw me. I was shifting big sacks about and he said, "Blimey, do you have to move these sacks by hand? You don't have to do that. Why don't you come over to us? There's none of that lark down there." So I went down to see them and got a job with them.'

The effect of full employment can be illustrated by what has happened to jobs with local authorities. They used to be highly prized, not·so much for the wages as for the security, which at the time counted more than anything else. Fathers employed by a Council accordingly did all they could to get their sons and relatives taken on as well. Some Council workmen still hold the sentiments of those days. A father who had spent his life working as a lavatory attendant for a neighbouring Council had a 'very good job', because it was safe, with a pension at the end of it, and his son, whom he had introduced to the same career, had done very well for himself, rising to become a 'foreman of lavatories'. Though family influence was usually exercised informally, the claims of kinship were in one respect recognized officially by local authorities: certain jobs, as attendants in women's lavatories, baths, and wash-houses, were more or less reserved for the widows of Council employees. 'They had widows down the latrines then.' Although there is now less demand from widows, this practice still continues.

But for most people the Council is not the prize it was. Security does not now matter enough to offset the low pay. Mr Sanderson, a dustman, explained how far his job had sunk. His father got it for him to start with: 'in those times it was father to son and all that caper' and lucky he was to get it. 'It was a respected job. You had to pass the doctor twice for fitness. I used to follow the horses and clear up the streets after them. You had to be recommended then to get it at all.' Times have changed.

'Things have got so bad that they recently started about a dozen black men. They've got the rough and rebel from everywhere. One of the black men was sweeping roads with a cardboard box with eyeholes over his head. The foreman asked him what he was doing that for and he said "Well guv'nor, it's cold." If it's a bad winter, they'll pack up, go home, and make rum.'

Today 'no one wouldn't bring any of their relatives here.'

Most municipal departments are now so short of labour they would welcome almost any relative of one of their existing employees. The position is not the same as with houses. Since there is no competition for jobs as rubbish-collectors and street-sweepers, this is not nepotism. The 'speaking for' system, in so far as it works at all, has a measure of official encouragement.

FATHER-SON SUCCESSION

This system probably used to result in many more sons following their fathers than do so today. We do not know;[1] we can only surmise. All we are certain about is that only ten out of the forty-five husbands in the Bethnal Green marriage sample have the same occupations as their fathers, as dockers, market porters, and in a few other trades. Although the numbers are so small, it is worthwhile looking at the individual examples because it appears that, in some more highly-regarded jobs, father-son succession is not just accident, but recognized practice. The informal 'speaking for' procedure has, it seems, been embodied in certain formal economic institutions, through the trade unions who have here supported the kinship principles observed by their members. We will consider in turn the three instances of docks, markets, and printing.

It is not new for sons of dockers to follow their fathers. Since it does not actually border the river, Bethnal Green is not a dockland community, but many local men have been employed in docks all the same. It is a matter of pride to belong to a docker's family. Mr Sandeman related that his father was a docker, his father's brothers, and his grandfather, an old man of seventy who is still working regularly. 'He's always laughing. He's got a fringe, a short haircut like they used to have in the old-fashioned days. He's a very jolly man.' Mr Sandeman got himself a job as a docker as soon as possible after he was demobilized. Mr Sykes was

1. By an oversight we omitted to ask about the occupations of the fathers of men subjects in the general sample.

another with a family connexion over several generations.[1]
'My father got me into it. You have to get a union ticket
first and then you get on the register. My father, my brother,
and me work in the same section, usually in the same gang.
My other brother works nearby.' Before the war, we were
told, fathers not only got their sons jobs but trained them
too. 'They kicked their sons' arses until they did lay the
ropes right. The son was the father's mate. He carried his
son while he was learning, and the sons later on carried
their fathers when they were old.'[2] The men were either
organized in family gangs, the oldest of them usually being
the ganger in charge, or belonged to different gangs but
helped their relatives when they could. There were many
well-established families – in a nearby dock, one of them
was, for instance, known as the 'Flying Eighteen', a group
of brothers and uncles with legendary sensitivity to the
'jungle drum beats which let them know a ship was coming
up the Thames'. One of them at least would be at the berth
seeking work before the ship docked, and, that done, would
send round for his relatives to make up the gang.

Since the war, labour has been 'decasualized' and a
guaranteed week introduced under the auspices of the National Dock Labour Board, a body appointed by the Government. The Board has maintained the traditional system of
recruitment. It notifies certain vacancies to the Transport
and General Workers' Union which calls upon its dock
branches to submit nominations. By long-standing custom –

1. A study of the Manchester docks reports that 'The Port of
Manchester is not yet old enough for more than three generations of the
same family to be connected with it; even so, 75 per cent of the dock
workers interviewed were sons of dock workers. About 10 per cent of the
men interviewed had entered the docks when they married dock
workers' daughters; some were themselves dock workers' sons but had
been introduced into dock work by their fathers-in-law or brothers-in-
law, rather than by their own fathers. This was most frequent where
the husband had gone to live with his wife's family on marriage.'
The Dock Worker, pp. 49–50.

2. The importance of inheritance of skill from fathers to sons was noted
in one of the best books ever written on the family. See Bosanquet, H.
The Family, pp. 207–17.

and it is custom only, this procedure not being written in to union agreements – the branches nominate only the sons of members, unless there are too few of these to go round. The difference from pre-war is that fewer sons now wish to follow their fathers. Families have moved away from the docks – partly owing to the growth of the housing estates, partly owing to the guaranteed week which has meant registered dock workers no longer have to live close to the job. Once they have moved, sons no longer go into the family trade as a matter of course. Men are not admitted to the industry until they are twenty-one, and by that time some of them, having a wide range of other jobs to choose from, have settled for other work. The old pride of calling (as the job is described) has by no means died out, but it is less intense now that some dockers' sons can see the virtue in other jobs which would at one time have been thought much inferior.

Plenty of fathers still want their sons to carry on the family tradition. Mr Tonks, a Greenleigh informant, was one of them. His grandfather and great-grandfather were dockers; so are most of his uncles, his brother, and his wife's brother. As for his son,

'I'm going to try and make my son a waterman – it's a skilled trade. I've applied to the union branch and with any luck he'll be taken on as an apprentice when he's fifteen and by the time he's twenty he'll have a good trade in his hands. He'll even have to get a certificate for swimming. The wages for watermen and lightermen aren't much better than dockers, but they're more regular. It's a more secure job.'

But his son was only thirteen. On a housing estate many miles from the river he cannot hear the sirens sound as the ships dock in the evening. He goes to school with very few other children from similar families. Even though he would be more skilled than his father, he may not be content to be a waterman.

Father-son succession, although not so widespread as it was, is still fairly common. The National Dock Labour

99

Board reported in 1950: 'There is keen competition to secure a place on the docks. The tradition of the job passing from father to son continues; out of 6,425 men recruited during the two years, 3,369 were dockers' sons.'[1] In London the proportion of dockers' sons wishing to follow their fathers is higher than elsewhere, because the docks have less purely seasonal trade and, therefore, more regular employment at full wages all the year round than most of the provincial ports. The extent of succession is noted in Table 12.

TABLE 12: Recruitment of Sons to London Docks[2]

(New Admissions to Main Register)

	1950	1951	1952	1953	1954
Dockers' sons	1208	2771	173	110	906
Others	254	1024	152	169	358

It is doubtful whether family succession is as prevalent in many other industries today.

The Transport and General Workers' Union plays much the same part in the big food markets, Billingsgate for fish, Covent Garden and Spitalfields for fruit and vegetables, and Smithfield for meat. In new recruitment of market porters, the Union gives preference to members' sons just as it does in the docks.

'Portering's a family game,' said Mr Robbins. 'My father's been a meat porter for more than fifty years. You grow up to it. You hear all about market work when you're a boy. I started work in Smithfield before I went into the Army and then when I came out of the Army I went back to work there again. That's where my family is.'

At Covent Garden, particularly, there jostles with the family tradition another one, which apparently dates from the erstwhile presence there of the National Sporting Club.

1. *Review of the Work of the National Dock Labour Board, 1947-1949*, pp. 18–19.
2. This information was kindly supplied by the National Dock Labour Board.

The 'gentry' used to attend the boxing to lay wagers on the porters who fought there after their work was done. A man with skill as a boxer, and a 'tin ear' (cauliflower ear) to prove it, had such prestige that he might be able to gain entry even though he was not son to the right father. This happened to Mr Haddon, one of our informants who had once been a near-professional boxer. 'Of course, in those days,' he told us, 'it wasn't easy to get a licence because there was all that business of fathers speaking for their sons and all that. I had to fight my way in. The big fellows there boss the others around and say, "Go on, eff off," and all that. There was one big fellow there and I decided that the only way to get anywhere was to have a go with him. I thought, "Right, you'll do for me." So I went up and started talking to him – I talked respectable like, I talked to him nicely, you know, and he started shouting and effing, so I said "Righto." We took our coats off and we had a fight. All the market stopped – there was hundreds of people round watching. Well, we had the fight – and I won. I got two black eyes myself, but I won – and after that all the people were asking what my name was and were offering me the good jobs.' This was rare, and a union official told us that at least 90 per cent of the men taken on in the markets before the war were porters' sons. By now the proportion has fallen to not much more than half the total recruitment.

The same practices also rule in 'the print'. Though we did not have in our sample skilled printers, we did have one who had obtained a job in one of the less skilled trades. The union which he had been able to join, through his brother, was the National Union of Printing, Bookbinding, and Paper Workers. Its official journal refers from time to time to the 'members' sons and brothers list', in such terms as: 'The members' sons and brothers list is again being opened. . . . Members of the London Central Branch who have sons and brothers of twenty-one and over whose names they wish to place on the list, should make immediate application for a form . . .'[1] Mr Trent explained:

1. *The Paperworker*, Vol. I, No. 10, February 1953, p. 22.

'I got it because my brother was working at the *Daily* —. You can't get on to the union unless you've got somebody already working there. They give it out at the paper for fathers and sons and brothers. He put my name down and the union let me know when they had a job. It's a closed shop, like.'

LINK BETWEEN THE MEN

In the docks, the markets, and in printing the right to family succession has been formally acknowledged. The same system, we would expect, works sporadically and less formally right through the economy of East London, and in all probability far beyond that. We came across plenty of other examples in our district, especially where there was heritable property – of shops where 'Brown & Son' meant what it said, of newspaper sellers who had inherited their 'pitches', of costermongers who had worked with their families because, in a business where confidence is essential, they did not have enough faith in anyone else. We have a vivid memory of the street rag-dealer who gave us a long and precise account of the effect of changes in supply and demand upon the prices of rags and, incidentally, said that 'Rags is a recognized rogue's trade. The trade is so tricky you can't trust anyone unless they're a relative.'

Wherever father works with son and brother with brother, the men have a link the counterpart of the women's. Family and workplace are intertwined. When there is a quarrel at work, it spreads over into the family.

'My husband went to work for his brother Jim. Jim was a fore-man scaffolder. Once when I was in hospital with a burnt hand, he came to see me and was late for work. Harry told him off and they had a tiff over it. My husband left and branched off on his own and we never see Jimmy any more.'

And where there is harmony at work it also spreads over into the family. Men who work with fathers or with brothers naturally see them every weekday, and often see a good deal of them when off work as well. Mr Aves, for instance, not content to work alongside two brothers and a brother-in-law in the same small building firm, sees them continuously at week-ends too.

'I see one of my brothers every Saturday at football, and then every Sunday the whole family comes down for a drink on Sunday morning. They've always done it. The men, my brothers and brothers-in-law, go round to the pub and then the women get the dinner cooked and come round for the last half hour for a chat and a drink. Oh, it's a regular thing in our family.'

In such families men at work may be as much centred on kinship as women at home, and when this happens, each can well understand and sympathize with the attachments of the other. Some of the men who most fully accepted their wives' close association with their mothers were in fact almost as closely tied, through the workplace, to their own blood relatives. The lives of both were shaped to the same pattern.

There are almost certainly fewer men of this sort than there used to be. When unemployment was rife, the kindred constituted an informal union within the formal trade union structure. Many relatives to speak for you were a better standby than any labour exchange. Today their importance is less. Now that men can get jobs of their own choosing without being introduced by relatives, it is becoming more rare for sons to follow a family tradition. Less than a quarter of our husbands (as we saw) had the same occupation as their fathers. But all our wives had the same work as their mothers.

7
KINSHIP AND COMMUNITY

WE have, in the part of the book which is here to be ended, moved successively outwards from the married couple to the extended family, from the extended family to the kinship network, and from there to certain of the relations between the family and the outside world. We shall now turn from the economic to the social, and consider whether, outside the workplace, people in this particular local community unrelated either by marriage or by blood are related in any other way.

Since family life is so embracing in Bethnal Green, one might perhaps expect it would be all-embracing. The attachment to relatives would then be at the expense of attachment to others. But in practice this is not what seems to happen. Far from the family excluding ties to outsiders, it acts as an important means of promoting them. When a person has relatives in the borough, as most people do, each of these relatives is a go-between with other people in the district. His brother's friends are his acquaintances, if not his friends; his grandmother's neighbours so well known as almost to be his own. The kindred are, if we understand their function aright, a bridge between the individual and the community: this will be the main theme of the chapter.

The function of the kindred can be understood only when it is realized that long-standing residence is the usual thing. Fifty-three per cent of the people in the general sample were born in Bethnal Green,[1] and over half those not born locally had lived in the borough for more than fifteen years. Most

1. A special analysis of the 1951 Census returns undertaken by the Registrar-General's staff showed that Bethnal Green had a higher proportion of residents born in it than did almost any other London borough.

people have therefore had time to get to know plenty of other local inhabitants. They share the same background. The people they see when they go out for a walk are people they played with as children. 'I've always known Frank and Barney,' said Mr Sykes. 'We was kids together. We knew each other from so high. We were all in the same street.' They are the people they went to school with. 'It's friendly here,' according to Mrs Warner. 'You can't hardly ever go out without meeting someone you know. Often it's someone you were at school with.' They are the people they knew at the youth club, fellow-members of a teen-age gang, or boxing opponents. They have the associations of a lifetime in common. If they are brought up from childhood with someone, they may not necessarily like him, they certainly 'know' him. If they live in the same street for long they cannot help getting to know people whom they see every day, talk to and hear about in endless conversation. Long residence by itself does something to create a sense of community with other people in the district. Even an unmarried orphan would have local acquaintances if he were established in this way. But, unmarried orphans being rare, as a rule a person has relatives also living in the district, and as a result his own range of contacts is greatly enlarged. His relatives are also established. Their play-mates and their school-friends, their work-mates and their pub-companions, are people whom he knows as well. Likewise, his friends and acquaintances also have their families in the district, so that when he gets to know any individual person, he is also likely to know at least some of his relatives.

The Bethnal Greener is therefore surrounded not only by his own relatives and their acquaintances, but also by his own acquaintances and their relatives. To show what this means in practice, let us accompany one of our informants on an ordinary morning's shopping trip. It lasted about half an hour. As she went along the street, nodding and chatting to this person and that, Mrs Landon commented on the people whom she saw.[1]

1. We are indebted for this account to Phyllis Willmott.

(1) MARY COLLINS. 'She's a sister of Sally who I worked with at the button place before I got married. My Mum knew her Mum, but I sort of lost touch until one day I found myself sitting next to her in Meath Gardens. We both had the babies with us and so we got talking again. I see quite a lot of Mary now.'

(2) ARTHUR JANSEN. 'Yes, I knew him before I was married. He worked at our place with his sister and mother. He's married now.'

(3) MAVIS BOOT. 'That lady there, I know her. She lives down our turning,' said Mrs Landon, as she caught sight in the butcher's of a back view of a large woman carrying the usual flat cloth bag. 'She's the daughter of one of Mum's old friends. When she died Mum promised to keep an eye on Mavis. She pops in at Mum's every day.'

(4) JOAN BATES is serving behind the counter at the baker's. 'She used to be a Simpson. She lives in the same street as my sister. My Mum knows her better than me.'

(5) SYBIL COOK. 'That's a girl I knew at school called Sybil.'

(6) KATIE SIMMONS. 'She's from the turning. Mum nursed her Mum when she was having Katie.'

(7) BETTY SALMON AND HER MOTHER. 'They live in the next turning to ours. Betty says she's had nothing but trouble with her daughter since she went to school.'

(8) RICHARD FIENBURGH. 'That man over there at the corner. He's a sort of relative. He's a brother of my sister's husband. He lives near them.'

(9) PATRICK COLLIS. This was a man in an old car parked by the shops. 'His mother lives in the turning.'

(10) AMY JACOBS is an old and bent woman who turns out to be Mrs Landon's godmother. 'Usually it's only when I'm with Mum that we talk.'

(11) SADIE LITTLE. This time there was not even a nod. The two women walked straight past each other. 'She's quarrelled with my sister so we don't talk to each other.'

(12) ALFRED CROSLAND. He is the father of the Katie seen a few minutes before.

(13) VIOLET BELCHER, a tall, thin lady talking to another at the street corner, is an 'acquaintance of Mum's. She's got trouble with her inside.'

(14) EMMA FRANCE. This was an elderly, very jolly woman, with grey hair and a loud laugh. She engaged Mrs Landon in conversation.

'How's that other sister of yours?'

'Lily?'

'Yes, your Mum told me. She's gone to live in Bow, hasn't she?'

'She's got a place with her mother-in-law there.'

'She don't like it? No! It never did work and I don't suppose it ever will.'

They both collapsed into laughter at this. Afterwards Mrs Landon explained that Mrs France had been her landlady in the first rooms her Mum had got for her.

That was just one unexceptional shopping trip. 'Some days', says Mrs Landon, 'you see so many you don't know which to talk to.' She kept a record over a week of all the people she saw in the street and whom she considered herself to 'know'. There were sixty-three people in all, some seen many times and thirty-eight of them relatives of at least one other person out of the sixty-three. Her story showed how she had built up a series of connexions with people she had known in school, work, or street, and, even more forcefully, how her mother and other kin acted as a means of communication between herself and the other people in her social world.

HOME AND STREET

We should make it clear that we are talking mainly about what happens *outside* the home. Most people meet their acquaintances in the street, at the market, at the pub, or at work. They do not usually invite them into their own houses.[1] We asked people whether they visited, or were visited by, friends in one or other home at least once a month.

1. This has been noticed before, in the course of research in the nearby borough of Greenwich. See Bakke, E. W. *The Unemployed Man*, pp. 153-4.

'Friend' was here defined as anyone other than a relative. Out of the ninety men and women in the marriage sample, eighty-four exchanged visits with relatives, and only thirty-two with friends. Those exchanging the most visits with relatives also did so with friends; those most sociable inside the family were also the most sociable outside. But the majority neither had, nor were, guests.

Several people said they had possessed many more friends when they were single. Marriage and children made the difference.

'Since we've had the children I've got no more friends – outside the family I mean.'

'I don't see my best friend much. She's married too, and she's always round *her* Mum's like I'm always round mine.'

'Since we've had the baby, I've got no men friends – outside the family, that is.'

The general attitude was summed up by Mr Jeffreys.

'I've got plenty of friends around here. I've always got on well with people, but I don't invite anyone here. I've got friends at work and friends at sport and friends I have a drink with. I know all the people around here, and I'm not invited into any one else's home either. It doesn't seem right somehow. Your home's your own.'

Where every front door opens on to street or staircase, and houses are crowded on top of one another, such an attitude helps to preserve some privacy against the press of people.

This exclusiveness in the home runs alongside an attitude of friendliness to other people living in the same street. Quite often people have themselves lived there for a long time – one out of every ten women and one out of every twenty men in the general sample still live in the street where they were born – and consequently know many of the other residents well. Quite often, too, either they or their neighbours also have relatives in the street who add to the spread of social contacts. If a person gets on bad terms with another person in the street – like Mrs Shipway whose neighbour 'started spreading stories about me and told me off for sending my children to Mum's when I go out to work' – she is also on bad terms with her family. 'They're all related in this street,' said Mr Lamb. 'It's awful, you can't talk to any-one in the street about any of the others, but you find it's a relation. You have to be very careful.'[1] But if he is careful and keeps on good terms with his neighbours, he is also on good terms with their relatives, and can nod to them in the street, knowing that he will get a response. He only has to stand at his front door to find someone out of his past who is also in his present.

'I suppose people who come here from outside think it's an awful place, but us established ones like it. Here you can just open the door and say hello to everybody.'

The streets are known as 'turnings', and adjoining ones as 'back-doubles'. Surrounded by their human associations, the words had a glow to them. 'In our turning *we*', they would say, 'do this, that, or the other.' 'I've lived in this turning for fifty years', said one old man proudly, 'and here I intend to stay.' The residents of the turning, who usually make up a sort of 'village' of 100 to 200 people, have their own places to meet, where few outsiders ever come – prac-tically every turning has its one or two pubs, its two or three shops, and its 'bookie's runner'. They organize their own parties: nearly every turning had its committee and cele-bration (and several built wooden stages for the display of local talent) for the Coronation of 1953. Some turnings have little war memorials built on to walls of houses with inscrip-tions like the following:

R. I. P.

IN LOVING MEMORY OF THE MEN OF CYPRUS STREET WHO MADE THE GREAT SACRIFICE
1914–1918
J. AMOS, E. AGOMBAR, A. BOARDMAN, A. H. COLE . . .

– there follow the names of the other twenty-two soldiers from Cyprus Street. Above it is a smaller plaque to the men

1. Publicans and shopkeepers also have to be cautious. If they fall out with one person they may lose as customers ten of his relatives as well.

killed in 1939–45: 'They are marching with their comrades somewhere on the road ahead.' Pots and vases of flowers are fixed in a half-circle to the wall; they are renewed regularly by the women of the turning, who make a street collection every Armistice Day.

There is the same kind of feeling in the few small courts still standing where a few houses face each other across a common front-yard. In one of these, the houses are covered from top to bottom with green trellis-work, tiers of window boxes stand out from the trellis, and on one wall is a proliferation of flowers around a war memorial, a Union Jack, and some faded pictures of the Queen. One of the residents told us, with evident satisfaction, that she was born in the same courtyard house that she had lived in for sixty-two years and spoke with slight disparagement of her neighbours: 'They're new here – they've only been here eighteen years.' She had been shocked to hear that the authorities might be labelling her beloved court a 'slum', and was now terrified lest they pull it down.

Robb, whose research was also done in Bethnal Green, cites an even more striking example.

'One informant who lived in a house that had been occupied by his parents and grandparents stated that he could not remember a new family coming into the street of seventy houses during the previous forty years.'[1]

THE VILLAGES OF THE BOROUGH

Sometimes a person's relatives are in the same turning, more often in another nearby turning, and this helps to account for the attachment which people feel to the precinct, as distinct from the street, in which they live. A previous observer remarked:

There is further localism within the borough. People are apt to look for their friends and their club within a close range. The social settlements draw nearly all their members from within a third of a mile, while tradition dictates which way borderline streets face for their social life. The main streets are very real social barriers, and

1. Robb, J. H. *Working Class Anti-Semite*, p. 57.

to some residents the Cambridge Heath Road resembles the Grand Canyon.[1]

In Bethnal Green, the one-time villages which have as elsewhere been physically submerged and their boundaries usually obliterated – Mumford talks of London as a 'federation of historic communities'[2] – live on in people's minds. Bow is one, Cambridge Heath another, Old Bethnal Green Road another, the Brick Lane area, once just outside the environs of the City, another. 'I reckon it's nice – this part of Bethnal Green I'm talking about,' remarked Mr Townsend. 'I'm not talking of Brick Lane or that end. Here we're by Victoria Park.' 'It's all right on this side of the canal,' said Mrs Gould, who lives in Bow. 'I wouldn't like to live on the other side of the canal. It's different there.' Another man, in a letter asking for help in getting another home, wrote 'I am not particular where you send me, the farther the better. I do not mind if it is as far as Old Ford as I have left my wife and wish to keep as far away as possible.' Old Ford is five minutes' walk from his wife. Other researchers have reported how difficult it was to get people to move even in the war.

Many stories were told of families who would rather camp in the kitchens of their uninhabitable blitzed houses or sleep in public shelters than accept accommodation in another area of the borough.[3]

When people have to move away from one part of the borough to another, they can appreciate the difference. Mr Gould, when he married, moved away from his parents and went about ten minutes' walk away to live near his wife's parents elsewhere in the borough, in this case in Bow. 'I'd like to be back in Bethnal Green,' he said, 'I would really. In Bethnal Green we have good neighbours, better than those in Bow I can tell you.' Mrs Tawney had moved as unwillingly in the other direction.

1. Self, P. J. O. 'Voluntary Organizations in Bethnal Green', p. 236.
2. Mumford, L. *City Development*, p. 190.
3. Glass, R. and Frenkel, M. 'How they live at Bethnal Green', p. 43.

'We're both from Bow. We're not very well known around here. We've only lived here since we got married, you see. In Bow you knew everybody, grew up with everybody, everybody recognized you. Over here they're a bit on the snobbish side – they know you're a stranger and treat you like one. They cater for you more in Bow. You like the place where you're mostly born, don't you?'

People who have moved know that their old neighbours would still stand by them if necessary. Mrs Jeffreys told us that in Ramsgate Street, where she had lived all her life until she was bombed out in 1944, even now, over ten years later, 'They all know Edith Jeffreys. Any of them'll give me a character.'

When there is such localism within the borough it is not surprising that for a few people places beyond Bethnal Green are another world. One woman had never been outside the borough except for an odd visit to the 'Other End', as the West End of London[1] is known locally. Another never left the borough except for the usual day-trip once a year to Southend. Yet another said 'I only went out once when we went to Canvey just before the war. I felt very strange and lonely when I went there. I've never been out of Bethnal Green since except once to go to Southend for the day.' Many of the most rooted people do not talk about fares but about 'riding fares', and while we do not know the origin of the term, in context it sometimes suggested that to pay a fare to travel anywhere was something outlandish and even a little daring. One man said that his aged mother was in an Old People's Home 'over the water'. 'Over the water' meant over the Thames, a mile or two away in Southwark.

In Bethnal Green the person who says he 'knows every-one' is, of course, exaggerating, but pardonably so. He does, with various degrees of intimacy, know many people outside (but often through) his family, and it is this which makes it, in the view of many informants, a 'friendly place'. Bethnal

1. Some people regard the West End as an immoral place which good East Londoners should not frequent. In some parts of the East End the last bus at night from the West End was ironically known not so long ago as the 'virgin's bus'. See Matthews, W. *Cockney Past and Present*, p. 143.

Green, or at any rate the precinct, is, it appears, a community which has some sense of being one. There is a sense of community, that is a feeling of solidarity between people who occupy the common territory, which springs from the fact that people and their families have lived there a long time. We cannot do better than put it in our informants' own words.

'Well, you're born into it, aren't you? You grow up here. I don't think I'd like to live anywhere else. Both my husband and me were born here and have lived here all our lives.'

'You asking me what I think of Bethnal Green is like asking a countryman what he thinks of the country. You understand what I mean? Well, I've always lived here, I'm contented. I suppose when you've always lived here you like it.'

THE LINK THROUGH HISTORY

The family contributes in another way to this sense of community, by giving people a very personal link with its past. People's parents and sometimes even their grandparents were born in Bethnal Green.

'I was bred and born in Bethnal Green and my parents and their parents before them: no, I wouldn't leave Bethnal Green, I wouldn't take a threepenny bus ride outside Bethnal Green.'

In such families local history does not have to be learnt from books: it is passed on by word of mouth from parents to children. Mr Firth probably had not read that Pepys once came to Bethnal House and had 'a fine merry walk with the ladies alone after dinner in the garden'.[1] But he related with a certain satisfaction that:

'My father used to tell me about the old days when sheep were grazing where Victoria Park Gardens are now laid out and Cambridge Heath Road was still fields. At week-ends my father was a keeper at the Burial Ground. It's in Defoe; there's a book on it, father knew all about it.'

The past lives on most tellingly in the families of French descent. Almost everyone in Bethnal knows about the Huguenots.

1. Quoted by Rose, M. *The East End of London*, p. 16.

The economy stems from the early silk weavers. The love of birds, animals, and flowers, which to this day makes some backyards a glory of bright colour, is said to be due to their influence. The Society for Protestant Refugees from High and Low Normandy still flourishes and serves many local people who could not claim French blood. But in the Huguenot families – and especially those with the French names which still stand out on the electoral rolls – the connexion is a source of special pride.

They rarely have documentary evidence of their ancestry. One local informant not in the sample was exceptional: he brought out an old paper written in somewhat strange French in the year of the Revolution, which as far as could be made out was a petition from a man who was his ancestor beseeching the Governors of the French Hospital in Hackney to employ, and at the same time treat, his granddaughter. Others did not know the details of their genealogies, nor were they even sure of their relationship to other local people of the same name. Mr Michaud thought that some other people were the offspring of his paternal great-uncle, but they were 'not quite up to Mum's and Dad's standard'. Mr Berthot told us that he had once by accident met a girl who was probably a relative. 'Once a girl came up to me at work and said "You look just like my Dad, what's your name?" ' It turned out that her name too was Berthot.' But though the details were hazy, they did claim to come of Huguenot stock – as one man put it, 'My people came over from Lyon with the weavers.' For them, and to a lesser extent for other local residents, the fact that their 'people' as well as themselves were born in Bethnal Green helps to keep alive a very personal sense of history, and this sense of history reinforces the feeling of attachment (just as it does in a regiment, a university, a trade union, or a political party) to the community and to its inhabitants.

KINSHIP AND RESIDENCE: IN CONCLUSION

We started this chapter by inquiring – In the lives of Bethnal Greeners is kinship all? Is there any room for others than relatives? The answer is tentative. We did not ask in our interviews as closely or systematically about non-relatives as about relatives. But we left with the impression that the kindred, far from being a barrier, are in fact a doorway to the community. Some people do, no doubt, enclose themselves completely within the family; many do not willingly admit any but family to the privacy of their homes; most have no friend who takes pride of place over close relatives. But in general, it seems, relatives do not compete with friends, rather act as intermediaries with them. We said in the Introduction that each of the relatives in a person's family of origin is a link with yet another family, and so on in a widening network, 'each family of marriage being knitted to each family of origin and each family of origin to each family of marriage by a member that they have in common'. Our present proposition is that each of the relatives in the families of origin, and indeed in the network as a whole, is a link not only with other families but with people outside the family as well.

In itself this is only a formal proposition, just as the original proposition was formal. To say that there is a 'link' (a clumsy metaphorical term, we admit) is not to say anything about its character. We have to inquire what actually happens between the family and the outside world, that is, into the nature of the 'links', just as we have to inquire what actually animates the formal structure of the family. Our belief is that in Bethnal Green the links, with a mother who lives in the next street and hence with her friends, acquaintances, and enemies, are more continuously effective because of the proximity to her and of the length of time for which proximity has existed.

The interaction between length of residence and kinship is therefore the crux of our interpretation. Neither is by itself a sufficient explanation. People in their families of marriage, let us suppose, live for a long period in one district without being related to others. They will establish many common associations through having children at the same schools, through meeting in the same shops, and through travelling on the same trains. But since there are no related families in the locality they will not be able to make use of the kind of social connexion which we have described. People could also, let us suppose, migrate in a caravan of related families. They would then have relatives around them, but these relatives would not be able to introduce them to so many outside the family precisely because none of them would be rooted in the district. Either length of residence or localized kinship does something to create a network of local attachment, but when they are combined, as they are in Bethnal Green, they constitute a much more powerful force than when one exists without the other. Then people have a number of links, or ways of orienting themselves, to the same person: he was at school, he is a relative by marriage, he lives in a well-known neighbourhood. Then people can make use of one or other of their possible approaches to establish a relationship with almost anyone, one might say to get a 'bearing' on almost anyone. We only make these distinctions in order to clarify the interpretation. In practice it must be very rare to find long residence without local kinship or local kinship without long residence.

In this old-established district the relatives are a vital means of connecting people with their community. We do not suggest that family is the only doorway to friendship; by taking account of the associations of school and work we have tried to keep a balance between kinship and the rest. Certainly, many friends of whom informants spoke were made by them quite independently, at school, at work, or in the army. But here the family does more than anything else to make the local society a familiar society, filled with people who are not strangers. This has its disadvantages. If you know other people's business, they know yours. Feuds may be all the more bitter for being contained in such small space. But there are advantages too. For many people, familiarity breeds content. Bethnal Greeners are not lonely people: whenever they go for a walk in the street, for a drink in the pub, or for a row on the lake in Victoria Park, they know the faces in the crowd.

*

In ending this chapter we also conclude the first part of the book. If we are to pick out one conclusion, it is the importance of residence. The Bethnal Greeners whom we have been describing did not change their residence just because they got married. They have remained in their district, and consequently in their families, of origin. The wife stays close to her mother because she already shares so many common interests and associations, and since she stays nearby, she keeps them alive and renews them. The wife's relationship most of all with her mother, but also with her other female relatives, is firmer than the husband's relationship with his men relatives, unless indeed he works with them. But the husband, while he may move towards his wife's home, does not usually move far from his own parents; he maintains his connexion with them at the same time as he does in the ordinary way succeed in resolving the tension between himself and his in-laws.

A special cast is given to all these adjustments and re-adjustments by the fact that they are played out within a limited physical space. Relatives in a double sense close cannot easily avoid each other: they either quarrel or merge at least part of their lives. Where mother and daughter are also neighbours they are almost bound to share with each other the tasks which fall to women, and this despite the many changes in housing, in the child welfare services, in the birth-rate, and, above all, in the relationship between man and wife.

We have stressed the bearing of residence, in its time dimension, upon family ties and upon the friendliness of unrelated people. But have we not, here as elsewhere, perhaps overdone its importance? The best way to test our impressions is to watch what happens when people change their residence. We cannot, as research sometimes can, induce an experimental change and observe the results. We cannot select a sample of people and persuade them to move for the sake of our strange mission. The best we can do is to follow ex-Bethnal Greeners who have recently moved out of the borough to a housing estate and select from the migrants a sample similar to the people upon whom we have focused so far. In the next chapters we follow some couples from Bethnal Green to Greenleigh.

PART TWO

FAMILIES ON THE MOVE

8

FROM BETHNAL GREEN
TO GREENLEIGH

Less than twenty miles away from Bethnal Green, the automatic doors of the tube train open on to the new land of Greenleigh. On one side of the railway are cows at pasture. On the other, the new housing estate. Instead of the shops of Bethnal Green there is the shopping centre at the Parade; instead of the street barrows piled high with fruit, fish, and dresses, instead of the cries of the costermongers from Spitalfields to Old Ford, there are orderly self-service stores in the marble halls of the great combines. In place of the gaunt buildings rising above narrow streets of narrow houses, there are up-to-date semi-detached residences. Bethnal Green encases the history of three hundred years. Cottages built for the descendants of Huguenot refugees, with their wide weavers' windows and peeling plaster, stand next to Victorian red-brick on one side and massive blocks of Edwardian charity on the other. Greenleigh belongs firmly to the aesthetics of this mid-century. Built since the war to a single plan, it is all of one piece. Though the Council has mixed different types of houses, row upon row look practically identical, each beside a concrete road, each enclosed by a fence, each with its little patch of flower garden at front and larger patch of vegetable garden at back, each with expansive front windows covered over with net curtains; all built, owned, and guarded by a single responsible landlord.

Instead of the hundred fussy, fading little pubs of the borough, there are just the neon lights and armchairs of the Merchant Venturer and the Yeoman Arms. Instead of the barrel organ in Bethnal Green Road there is an electrically amplified musical box in a mechanical ice-cream van. In place of tiny workshops squeezed into a thousand backyards rise the first few glass and concrete factories which will soon give work to Greenleigh's children. Instead of the sociable squash of people and houses, workshops and lorries, there are the drawn-out roads and spacious open ground of the usual low-density estate. Instead of the flat land of East London, the gentle hills of Essex.

'When I first came,' said Mrs Sandeman, 'I cried for weeks, it was so lonely. It was a shock to see such a deep hill going up to the shops.'

We chose this estate for our inquiry because Greenleigh is, in the view of L.C.C. officials, fairly typical of the estates to which Bethnal Greeners have been moved. We should issue two warnings. Our informants were only from Bethnal Green and their experience may be different from that of other residents on the estate. Secondly, our sample was very small – we interviewed forty-seven out of a sample of fifty couples in 1953, and of these only forty-one were available for a second interview two years later in 1955.[1] Allowing for couples seen more than twice and wives seen separately as well as with their husbands, we interviewed people in their homes on 127 occasions. But since our information, as we would stress, related to less than fifty couples, the views we have formed are bound to be even more impressionistic than those we have already set forth.

Two of the husbands in the sample died between 1953 and 1955, so that attention is in fact focused upon 41 wives and 39 husbands. The men, like their counterparts in the Bethnal Green marriage sample,[2] are mostly manual workers, only 6 of them being employed in clerical or other non-manual occupations. The couples in the sample at Greenleigh are rather older than those in the Bethnal Green sample: the average age of the men in 1955 was 39, against 36 in Bethnal Green, and of the women 37, compared with 33. Their children are older too and there are more of them.

Greenleigh is only one of several terminal points for the

1. The method of selecting the sample is described in the Appendix.
2. In this and the next two chapters we shall be comparing the marriage samples in the two places. We shall simply refer to them as the 'Bethnal Green sample' and the 'Greenleigh sample'.

great migration from the city. Relatively few houses have been built since the war inside London. It was quicker to put them up on vacant ground than to clear encumbered sites; it was simpler to acquire the land; more space was left for those who stayed behind. This is not new. For three hundred years houses have been striding out over the green fields: Bethnal Green itself was a kind of seventeenth-century Greenleigh.[1] The difference is that whereas then it was private enterprise, now it is public: in this century, the London County Council has been the great architect of the new suburbs. Before the war it built at Dagenham an estate which has now become a large, prosperous town. Since 1945 more council estates have been opened, more farmlands covered over, more people joined the great exodus.

As Essex has swollen, the East End boroughs have shrunk. The Census report sums up the change:

> The greater part of the decline in 1931–51 has taken place since 1939 and a substantial amount of that relating to the central and dockside areas must be attributed to the destruction of property and large-scale evacuation of population which took place during the war years, and the planning policies of the post-war period which have so far encouraged new building outside rather than inside the County.[2]

The population of Bethnal Green has fallen sharply. From 108,000 in 1931 it dropped to 90,130 in 1939, and was then almost halved, after the first waves of air raids, to 47,330 in 1941. It recovered to 60,580 in 1948 when some of the evacuees had returned; and from that date the borough has again lost population to the housing estates, retaining only

1. Even before that the Government had shown concern with over-crowding. In the sixteenth century (when the population of London was about the same as pre-war Bethnal Green) Queen Elizabeth I in one proclamation asserted the need for control of building in London 'where there are such great multitudes of people brought to inhabit in small rooms, whereof a great part are seen very poor, yea, such as must live of begging, or by worse means, and they heaped up together, and in a sort smothered with many families of children and servants in one house or one small tenement.' Quoted Sinclair, R. *East London*, pp. 172–3.

2. *Census*, 1951, *County Reporter, London*, p. xii.

53,860 in 1955. Between 1931 and 1955 nearly 11,000 families, containing over 40,000 people were rehoused from Bethnal Green on L.C.C. estates, many of them outside the county.[1]

The migration has left its mark on Bethnal Green. It is common to hear shopkeepers and publicans say they are losing business as the exodus to Essex goes on. School teachers complain they will soon have no pupils, clergymen that their parishes are emptying. At annual meetings of the local Labour Party there is the familiar lament: 'Once again many of our active members have moved out during the year.' The housing estates are no longer Siberias to which other, unknown people are banished; they are real places, at the end of the tube line, where one's own relatives have made their home. More than half the people in the Bethnal Green marriage sample had relatives on one or other of the six scattered L.C.C. estates in Essex. When they visit relatives on the estates or stay with them, the experience widens their horizons and raises their aspirations. They see a new house, also a new way of life. When a woman who has lived all her life in 'buildings' or in three cramped rooms in a grubby terraced cottage, is proudly shown round 'my sister's lovely new house with a garden out at Hainault', it is small wonder that admiration is sometimes tinged with envy or that 'dear old Bethnal Green' seems shabbier when she gets back to it. One Bethnal Green informant actually dislikes visiting her sisters because 'it gives me the needle afterwards with my dark place'; another because 'it disheartens you to see them nice places and come back to this dump'. If municipal housing within Bethnal Green has been a catalyst of social change, how much more so – for those who stay as well as for those who go – are the new estates 'out in the country'. In recent times the biggest change in Bethnal Green is Greenleigh.

MOTIVES FOR MIGRATION

A migration such as this gathers its own momentum, people

1. *London Housing Statistics, 1954-55,* p. 93.

who have moved persuading others by their example. Some of our Greenleigh families followed in the train of kin. Mrs Mallows explained she used to live in a Council flat in Bethnal Green.

'I came out here to see my three sisters who've moved out here, and when I saw them all in their houses, I wanted to move out too, so we put an advert in a shop.'

Others took relatives with them or were joined by them after arrival. Mr Trent was one of those who had acted 'path-finder' to his parents and his brother. There had been a big change for him between the two interviews of 1953 and 1955.

'My Mum's moved to Greenleigh since you were here before. She used to live in flats in Bethnal Green. Iris (Mr Trent's thirteen-year-old daughter) does for her. She goes in twice a week; she clears the place out and runs errands. All the children go round there and help. And I help with the gardening and I decorated her house. My father came down too, and my brother Tom has moved to Greenleigh as well. He wants it for the children. It's a mutual exchange.'

Altogether we found that a third of the Greenleigh couples had relatives on the estate in 1955 – nine out of forty-one had parent or sibling on the husband's side or the wife's, and a further five had more remote relatives living there. Once one member of a family has made the move, he is a magnet for the others.

It was easy enough to understand the people who already had relatives on the estate: they moved partly so that they could be near them. But what about the others? We have shown in the first part of this book how embracing kinship can be in Bethnal Green. People's lives are of a piece with their relatives; they gain evident advantage, as they see it, from the companionship and help of the family circle. Why then should they be ready to move away from their kin and the neighbours they know? One possible explanation was that the migrants might have had weaker family ties anyway. If so, they would neither have been so attached to the society of Bethnal Green, nor liable to suffer so much loss by leaving it.

To test this possibility, we asked the wives in the Greenleigh sample how much they saw their mothers before they left the borough, and drew a comparison with the ones in the Bethnal Green sample. There was no appreciable difference between them. Both sets of wives, those on the estate as well as those still in the borough, saw their mothers about four times a week; and the husbands in the two places were similarly alike in the extent to which they saw *their* mothers.

Frequency of contact is, of course, not necessarily a measure of affection, and in fact two of the wives admitted to relief at escaping from the coils of kinship. 'I don't mind about relatives,' Mrs Morrow said. 'You can't always be with relatives. The further away, the better you are – there's no jealousy amongst family or anything then.' Mrs Young said about her brothers and sisters – 'I don't mind not seeing much of them. I'm better off not so near to them. You don't get on each other's nerves.'

Mrs Morrow and Mrs Young were exceptional. Most of the Greenleigh wives not only had seen their mothers a good deal, as much as other dutiful daughters, but also seemed sorry to leave them. We therefore return to the question: If the migrants did not have weaker kinship attachments than other people, why did they come? The main reason is quite simple. The attraction is the house. Our couples left two or three damp rooms built in the last century for the 'industrious classes', and were suddenly transported to a spacious modern home. Instead of the tap in the backyard, there was a bathroom with hot and cold water. Instead of the gas stove on the landing, a real kitchen with a sink and a larder. Instead of the narrow living room with stained wallpaper and shaky floorboards, a newly painted lounge heated by a modern solid-fuel grate. And instead of the street for their children to play in, fields and trees and open country.

The contrast is all the sharper because the new residents had, in the main, come from Bethnal Green's worst houses.

A minority got there by exchanging a house in Bethnal Green with a tenant who wanted to go back. But, in general, the L.C.C.'s view of who needed it most decided who went. Our informants were mostly at the top of the L.C.C.'s housing list – they were living in the most overcrowded or the most unhealthy houses in the borough – and that is why they were selected.

If they had any choice at all, it was between a house on an estate and a flat in the city.

'I was between two thorns,' said one of our informants still in the borough, 'I didn't want a flat but I didn't want to leave Bethnal Green.'

This was a sharp dilemma. It could not be resolved as Mrs Stirling would have liked – 'If we could take the house with us, we'd go back like a shot.' The migrants were mostly people who decided that a house was the unfortunate best. 'Flats are no good for children,' they said, or 'You do need a garden,' or

'Flats are all right if you believe in Communism – you only want communal feeding and it's all in.'

Who can wonder that people crowded into one or two poky rooms, carrying water up three flights of stairs, sharing a w.c. with other families, fighting against damp and grime and poor sanitation, should feel their hearts lift at the thought of a sparkling new house with a garden? 'When we first came we were thrilled,' said Mrs Lowie, explaining that their home in Bethnal Green had been so small that meals had to be eaten in relays. 'Back in Bethnal Green we had mice in two rooms,' said Mrs Sandeman. 'After that this seemed like paradise.' When Mrs Young and her husband and two children were living in two rooms, there was 'one toilet between five families' and the sink Mrs Young had to use was 'on the next floor up'. Mrs Windle was the same – 'We were very overcrowded – we had only two rooms. We had to go up and down stairs for every drop of water – to the wash-house outside.' All but a few of the families we saw had a similar tale to tell of their former homes.

BETTER FOR THE KIDDIES

The house is not the only attraction. Greenleigh, being 'in the country' has, for some of the residents, other advantages over Bethnal Green. 'Everything seems quieter here, more calmer,' said Mrs Vince. 'The fresh air hits you when you come out of the station.' Many people value the air and fields even more for their children than for themselves. Greenleigh is generally thought 'better for the kiddies'.

So even where they left their kin with regret, the people were not deserting family so much as acting for it, on behalf of the younger rather than the older generation. The couples were at a stage of life when they were facing both ways, having responsibilities towards their children as well as towards their parents. Faced with the choice, they felt they had to put the one before the other. Mrs Ames, for example, said, 'We came to Greenleigh for Bill's sake. He was very ill with diphtheria. He got it by drinking the drain water from the sinks of the two families living above us. On top of that he was born bronchial. It has done the boy good to be out here.' 'I would go back if it weren't for the children,' said another mother. 'The children's health comes first – we're here to study them.'

In some cases this emphasis on the children had been given special point by the experience of evacuation. Mothers and children were then introduced not only to the country-side but to a different standard of housing, and when they returned to Bethnal Green it seemed far more grim than it had ever done before. One man put his name down for a housing estate as soon as he was demobilized. His family had spent the war in Sussex. 'I didn't think it fair to my children,' he said, 'to come home to places like we had after four years of country life.' Whether or not ideas had been changed by experiences like this, a majority of informants thought that Greenleigh was a more suitable environment for children. Mrs Adams's reply, when asked whether she wanted to leave Greenleigh, was typical:

'I'd say no. I'd say that for the children's sake. They do love it here and it's so much better for them. But if it were for myself alone, I'd say yes.'

Mrs Sandeman neatly posed the issue as she saw it – a conflict between kinship and the interests of the children – when, explaining that 'money was getting tighter', she said:

'I don't even go to my Mum now. I haven't got the fare money. But you've got to put up with things if you want a place for your children. Your children come first, I say.'

And Mrs Pickles expressed a similar opinion:

'Mum likes me to go and see her. I used to be with her a lot. She missed me a lot at the beginning. But we had to think of the kiddies, didn't we?'

This issue is one which every couple had to face for themselves before they came, and did not necessarily resolve after they had arrived. Many migrants in fact decided that they had made the wrong decision, and left the estate, most of them to return to the East End. Altogether, from the opening of the Greenleigh estate until March, 1956, 26 per cent of the tenants who had come there moved away again. But the rate of removals has been gradually falling in recent years: the numbers leaving in any year, as a proportion of all tenants living on the estate at that March, rose to 7 per cent in 1951–2 and then began to fall again, reaching 5 per cent in 1955–6.[1] Those who remain are the ones who have decided that, on balance, the advantages of the estate outweigh its disadvantages.

To move or not to move – it is seldom an easy decision. Greenleigh has its attraction, but so too has Bethnal Green. The choice is such a difficult one because to leave the

1. The information was supplied by the L.C.C. Housing Department. The annual removal figures are lower than for similar L.C.C. estates before the war, presumably as a result of full employment which makes it easier for people to pay higher rents. On the Dagenham estate the annual rate of removal in 1932 and 1933 was between 10 per cent and 12 per cent (Young, T. *Becontree and Dagenham*, p. 240). On the Watling estate the average annual rate was more than 10 per cent between 1927 and 1936 (Durant, R. *Watling*, p. 16).

borough is usually to leave the relatives behind as well. What this means for new residents is the subject of the next chapter.

9

THE FAMILY AT GREENLEIGH

ONCE the family moves to the housing estate, the question
of how they came to be there has for them an academic
flavour, and for us the question now is the difference migration has made to them. Table 13 compares contacts with
relatives before leaving Bethnal Green with those in 1953
and 1955. It records the *total* contacts of husbands and wives
with parents and siblings on both sides: before he moved,
the average husband, for example, saw one or other of his
relatives on fifteen occasions in a week.

TABLE 13: Changes in Weekly Contacts
with Relatives after Migration

(Greenleigh sample – 39 husbands and 41 wives)

	Average number of contacts per week with own and spouse's parents and siblings		
	Before leaving Bethnal Green	Greenleigh 1953	Greenleigh 1955
Husbands	15.0	3.8	3.3
Wives	17.2	3.0	2.4

As one would expect, people saw very much less of relatives after moving to the estate. Some relatives, of course, if
they already lived on the estate, were seen more often, but
the general effect of this was slight, since under one-twen-
tieth of all parents and siblings (18 out of 382) were on the
estate even by 1955. Most relatives were seen less after the
move. To reveal what difference this made we must rely on
the accounts given in the interviews. Mr and Mrs Harper
were one of the couples. Before their move, they led
the kind of life we have described in the first part of this

book. The contrast between old and new has been sharp.

Mrs Harper, a stout, red-faced woman in her late thirties, had, like her husband, always lived in the same part of Bethnal Green before she went to Greenleigh in 1948. She came from a large family – six girls and two boys – and she grew up amidst brothers and sisters, uncles and aunts and cousins. When she married at eighteen, she went on living with her parents, and her first child was brought up more by her mother than by herself. As the family grew, they moved out to three rooms on the ground floor of a house in the next street. Their life was still that of the extended family. 'All my family lived round Denby Street,' said Mrs Harper, 'and we were always in and out of each other's houses.' When she went to the shops she called in on her mother 'to see if she wanted any errands'. Every day she dropped in on one sister or another and saw a niece or an aunt at the market or the corner shop. Her many long-standing acquaintanceships were constantly being renewed. People were always dropping in on Mrs Harper. 'I used to have them all in,' she told us, 'relations and friends as well.' At her confinements, 'all my sisters and the neighbours used to help. My sisters used to come in and make a cup of tea and that.' And every Saturday and Sunday night there was a family party at Mrs Harper's mother's place: 'We all used to meet there week-ends. We always took the kiddies along.'

That busy sociable life is now a memory. Shopping in the mornings amidst the chromium and tiles of the Parade is a lonely business compared with the familiar faces and sights of the old street market. The evenings are quieter too: 'It's the television most nights and the garden in the summer.' Mrs Harper knew no one when she arrived at Greenleigh, and her efforts to make friends have not been very successful: 'I tried getting friendly with the woman next door but one,' she explained, 'but it didn't work.' It is the loneliness she dislikes most – and the 'quietness' which she thinks will in time 'send people off their heads'.

Her husband is of a different mind. 'It's not bad here,' he says. 'Anyway, we've got a decent house with a garden, that's the main thing – and it's made all the difference to the children. I don't let the other people here get me down.' He still works in Bethnal Green – there are no jobs for upholsterers at Greenleigh. This has its drawbacks, especially the fares and the time spent travelling, but it means he is able to look in on his parents once a week and call about once a month on his wife's father and eldest sister – Mrs Harper's mother having died, 'the old man lives with Fanny'.

Mrs Harper herself seldom sees her relatives any more. She goes to Bethnal Green only five or six times a year, when one of her elder sisters organizes a family party 'for Dad'. 'It costs so much to travel up there,' she said, 'that I don't recognize some of the children, they're growing so fast.' Tired of mooching around an empty house all day, waiting for her husband and children to return, with no one to talk to and with the neighbours 'snobbish' and 'spiteful', Mrs Harper has taken a part-time job. 'If I didn't go to work, I'd get melancholic.' Her verdict on Greenleigh – 'It's like being in a box to die out here.'

Mrs Harper's story shows how great can be the change for a woman who moves from a place where the family is linked to relatives, neighbours, and friends in a web of intimate relationships to a place where she may talk to no one, apart from the children, from the moment her husband leaves for work in the morning until he comes home again, tired out by the journey, at seven or eight at night. It is not just that she sees less of relatives than before: as a day-to-day affair, as something around which her domestic economy is organized, her life arranged, the extended family has ceased to exist. Other women remarked on their sense of loss. 'When I first came I felt I had done a crime,' said Mrs Prince, 'it was so bare. I felt terrible and I used to pop back to see Mum two or three times a week.' 'It's your family, that's what you miss. If you're with your family, you've always got someone to help you. I do miss my family,' 'We do miss the relatives out here,' 'I miss my Mum,' others told us in similar vein.

The loss was not so keen for all. One took her mother with her, another her husband's mother, two had sisters on the estate. But for most of the women the move meant a sharp break with the full life they had previously shared with others. For example, when they lived in Bethnal Green, twenty-four of the forty-one wives had seen one or more women relatives daily: at Greenleigh in 1955 only three did so.

AFTER TWO YEARS

One reason for interviewing migrants on two occasions – with a two-year interval between – was to allow us to see how the family's relations with kin were altered by the passage of time. In quantitative terms, the average drop in contacts between 1953 and 1955, shown in Table 13, is slight. But behind the averages lie some changes for individual families which are worth reporting.

On the one hand, by 1955 some families saw more than they had done two years before of relatives who had since joined them on the estate. An example is Mrs Trent. Her parents-in-law moved to Greenleigh between the two phases of interviewing, and she saw her mother-in-law three times a week instead of once in three months.

On the other hand, some women had 'settled down' at Greenleigh in the two years and had loosened their ties with their old homes. One thing we noticed in 1953 was that six of the women were still continuing to shop in Bethnal Green as often as once a week. Food was still rationed then and they had not broken their registrations with the shops they knew so well in Bethnal Green. If they went to Bethnal Green to shop, they could see relatives at the same time. By 1955 only one of the wives was going up to Bethnal Green on a regular weekly shopping expedition, though others went occasionally to get clothing and other things cheaper there. 'I don't go up there for shopping now,' said Mrs Clive, 'not now we've got our own shopping centre here.' The effect this can have on meetings with kin was voiced by Mrs Rawson – 'I haven't seen my Aunt Ada for a long time. We used to be rationed in Bethnal Green and then I used to see her occasionally in the market, but not now.'

These women had gradually become less absorbed in Bethnal Green and more in Greenleigh. The Maggs family illustrates what 'settling down' can mean. In 1953 they described themselves as 'lodging' in Greenleigh; Mr and Mrs Maggs both went to London to work and their daughters (like a few other children in 1953, but none in 1955) to their old schools in London; now Mrs Maggs has had another child and is at home all day, while one of her daughters expects to be coming to work at the local glassworks as soon as it opens. Though Mrs Maggs says she feels 'lonely' and 'misses her relations', they are lodgers at Greenleigh no longer.

One link has not been broken by time – many of the husbands have continued to work in London. At Greenleigh there are local jobs in only a limited number of trades. There are few openings for tailors, cabinet makers, french polishers, dockers, or lorry drivers. In 1953, thirteen of the forty-seven husbands were working in the East End and a further nine in other parts of the County of London; by 1955 some individuals had changed one way or the other, and there were by then fifteen out of thirty-nine working in the East End and eight elsewhere in London. From the estate as a whole, more people were travelling to the East End in 1955 than in 1953.[1]

Since many men have to travel to the East End for their work, their contacts with relatives have in general fallen less since they moved to the estate than their wives'. The husband has to meet his fares out of an income already strained by the higher rent. But if he has to pay his fares anyway, he can not only get to work on the one ticket but to his relatives also, and in some ways their very presence at the other end of the line may relieve his daily journey. Mr Mallows finishes his work in Bethnal Green at five. At that time 'the guards are forcing people into those trains every night', so he goes to his father's, to have a cup of tea. When he has

1 This information was provided by the London Transport Executive.

finished that and had a chat, the rush-hour is over; there is even a chance of getting a seat. Mr Parker used to go home every day for his dinner before he moved to Greenleigh. He cannot get used to the sandwiches which he takes instead, so he often has a hot meal at home with his mother. He has to pay her but at least that is cheaper than any other way of getting a hot dinner. Other men still make a point, as they did in Bethnal Green, of calling each week on their mothers, or they see their fathers and brothers at work, or just 'bang into' uncles and aunts and cousins on their walk from tube station to workplace, or in their dinner break.

They do not keep up with their own relatives alone; they do so with their in-laws also. Mr Ellis, who works in Bow, visits his wife's mother regularly once a month. Mr Lowie works in Bethnal Green as a cabinet maker and has his mid-day meal every day with his wife's sister. Other husbands call regularly to pay into family clubs, more often run by their wives' relatives than their own. Mr and Mrs Adams belong to a Public House Loan Club, and Mr Adams 'calls in on a Friday to give my sister our Club money. She takes it and pays it in for us.'

In 1955, six of the forty-one wives were working in London also. Mr Marsh had been working in a shop in Bethnal Green in 1953 and had kept in touch with the relatives, particularly his own mother; by 1955 he had got a job in a shop at Greenleigh instead, but now his wife was working for London Transport. 'Being on the buses,' he pointed out, 'the wife sees her mother and my mother more than I do now.'

It is not so much the distance that makes visiting difficult for the other women as the cost. Time and again, wives lamented that they were so short of money that they could not afford to visit Bethnal Green as often as they would like. 'If the fares were cheaper you could afford to go more often and it wouldn't be so bad,' was Mrs Adams's verdict. 'The fares put the damper on visiting relations more than anything else.'

THE NEW PATTERN OF VISITING

Even so, few women were cut off entirely. If we exclude the mother actually living with her daughter at Greenleigh, the twenty wives whose mothers were alive were, in 1955, still seeing them on average just under once a fortnight. Mrs Young, although she does not like going back to London at all because she feels shut in and choked there, goes about once a month all the same because 'with your family it's only natural, you've got to see them'.

Visiting between relatives is sometimes a two-way affair. Migration can be something in which the kindred share, the house and garden belonging not only to the family who live in it, but also in a sense to their relatives as well. Mrs Soper, one of our Bethnal Green informants, said that every fortnight she takes her two children 'on the Underground down to my sister at Hainault. We have a nice afternoon out there. It's quite a little outing.' Mrs Berry's sister also appreciates the attractions of Greenleigh: 'She loves to come down here. She says it's better than going to Southend or somewhere like that.' But you don't go to Southend in the winter. When the days begin to draw in and the morning air is colder, so too is enthusiasm for an excursion to the windswept spaces of a housing estate. 'It's really a bit of an outing for them to come out here in the summer time,' Mr Parker explained, 'but we see all the relatives less in winter than in summer.'

In summer the most popular time for visiting is, of course, the week-end. On a Sunday morning in the summer dozens of people can be seen coming out of the station, many carrying bags of fruit and flowers, as one person said 'quite like hospital on a visiting day'. 'Last August Bank Holiday,' said Mrs Hall, 'we had fourteen relatives down here.' Visitors do not necessarily stay for only one day. Greenleigh is suitable for holidays as well as day excursions. Sometimes people told us, as Mrs Lowie did, 'Mum comes down to stay two or three times a year.' In Bethnal Green, the kindred are at hand every day of the week. At Greenleigh the family has to wait for summer, for week-ends, for holidays, before they appear. But people still feel themselves members of the wider family, reaffirm their membership of it when they attend family rituals like weddings, funerals, and

Christmas parties 'back home', and use key relatives to keep them informed. 'I go to see the wife's sister every week,' said Mr Vince who works in Bow, 'to find out if there are any messages or anything about other relatives.' Such round-about communication with the families of origin is probably all the more necessary to husbands and wives who now spend so much time on their own.[1]

The approach we have adopted so far in this chapter – looking mainly at changes in *contacts* with relatives – is only one way of measuring the impact of the move. Another approach is to inquire about *services*, to ask what help the family gets on the housing estate compared with Bethnal Green. What happens, for instance, when the family faces extra problems – when the wife is incapacitated by illness or confinement?

CARE IN ILLNESS

Even those Greenleigh wives whose homes had not been visited by sickness had considered the prospect with misgiving. If husbands were away from work their families had to make do on a small sickness benefit, sometimes paid tardily at that.

'Last year my husband was off work and the health money took ages to come down. I told the rent collector and he said "That's no excuse." "Well, what am I to do," says I, "the health money's not come down. You know how long it always takes out here." Then on top of it all if I didn't have a saucy letter from them saying I'd missed a week's rent. It's above the limit, isn't it?'

Families with savings exhausted them. Families without had to borrow from relatives. The Todds would have been in an even worse state without help from the wife's father.

'When we first came my husband got ill with shingles. Because of the moving there was a muddle-up over the panel money and we

1. See also pp. 80-1

didn't get it for four weeks. So we had to borrow from my father and give everything up in order to pay the rent. On top of that there was the funeral money we had to borrow because when we first came we had to cash in all the insurance policies he had when he was ill and so we didn't get any money for the baby's funeral. We had to pay back father for that as well as the rest he lent us.'

When the husband was ill, his wife looked after him. When the wife was ill, who looked after her? We asked wives at Greenleigh, as in Bethnal Green, who was the main person helping them with the home and children when they were last ill in bed. At Greenleigh there was, of course, less help from relatives. Of the twenty-four Bethnal Green wives who had been ill, twelve had been helped during their sickness by relatives, eight of them by their mothers; but of the twenty-one wives at Greenleigh who had been ill since going there, only four had help from relatives, two from their mothers. One of these two was Mrs Chortle whose mother was living with her; the other was Mrs Windle, who was ill in bed for three days with tonsillitis.

'I stayed off the first day to look after the children. Then I couldn't stay off any longer,' said her husband. 'So I phoned up a neighbour in Wembley to tell her Mum. She came down for the next two days and stayed. It didn't cost her much because she had a privilege ticket, Dad being on the railway.'

Mrs Tonks's sister also came down when she was ill. The other wife who received help got it from her aunt living on the estate.

If relatives were too far away, who did it instead? Four people out of the twenty-one at Greenleigh (compared with four out of the twenty-four in Bethnal Green) had help from neighbours, six from husbands. Husbands might have done more but for the fear of losing the wages which were all the more needed in time of illness. The consequences could be serious if they did.

'My husband had to stop away from work when I was taken ill last time. He went to the Assistance Board and they said if you're still out in four weeks come back again. We'll never go there again.

It was the first time we needed money and still we didn't get any back for all we'd paid in. Bet's club (a family club in Bethnal Green) is better; you can depend on that.'

At all costs he had to bring in the money.

'My husband lost three days but then he had to go back because we couldn't do without the money. The doctor said I was supposed to stay in bed a week but I had to get up. I got an abscess in the breast because I got up too soon.'

In Bethnal Green, people with relatives close by seldom go short of money in a crisis like this. If they do not belong to a family club from which they can draw a loan, some relative will lend them money. Borrowing from relatives is often more difficult at Greenleigh. 'You notice the difference out here,' said Mr Tonks, 'when you fall on hard times. Up there you were where you were born. You could always get helped by your family. You didn't even have to ask them – they'd help you out of trouble straight away. Down here you've had it.' 'That's why families stick together,' said a Bethnal Green husband. 'If you're short of money you can always go round your Mum and get helped out.'

At Greenleigh the shortage of money drives the men back to work – leaving the responsibility to the children. The main difference between the two places was that wives depended more on their children – seven out of twenty-one were looked after by them, as compared with two out of twenty-four at Bethnal Green. 'When I was ill, my eldest daughter stayed at home from work and looked after me,' said Mrs Berry, and her husband confessed his own helplessness when he added, 'When Mum's ill, Dad's ill as well, you know what I mean? I wasn't a bit of use myself; I don't know how we'd have managed if it hadn't been for Shirley.'

Children younger than Shirley stayed away, not from work, but from school. When Mrs Painswick went to hospital her eldest daughter, then aged eleven, stopped at home to look after her younger brother and sister. Her aunt visited the home to see if everything was all right and afterwards came to the hospital to report that her daughter was managing very well – 'everything was spotlessly clean.' Even so Mrs Painswick worried continuously. Mrs Rawson suffered too.

'I got such a chill through leaving off my underslip that I nearly took the cow's way out. I had to keep Billy back from school. I broke down having to do that. Billy did the shopping and paid the rent man and I struggled to do the cooking.'

The question about help at childbirth showed the same decline in dependence on relatives. Of the wives at Green-leigh, nineteen had had their last child since they moved to the estate, and Table 14 compares the help given to them at their confinement with that given to the wives in the Bethnal Green sample. We asked who looked after the older child or children while the wife was confined, whether this was at home or in hospital.

TABLE 14: Care of Children at Last Confinement

(*Marriage samples compared*)

Person caring for older child(ren)	Bethnal Green sample	Greenleigh sample
Relatives	29	4
Husband, children, or neighbours	15	15
TOTAL	44	19

The Bethnal Green total excludes one family in which the only other child was ill in hospital at the time of confinement. The Greenleigh total is of all the wives who had been confined since their arrival on the estate

The kindred of Bethnal Green were no longer predominant. Out of the twenty-nine wives in Bethnal Green helped by relatives at their confinement, eighteen were helped by their mothers: at Greenleigh only one wife was – the Mrs

Chortle whose mother lives with her.[1] Of the remaining three relatives, two were living at Greenleigh, and one came out to stay. Of the other fifteen families, neighbours helped only five; one family turned to a Home Help; seven husbands stayed off work; and in two families the children looked after themselves.

In day-to-day affairs, too, neighbours rather rarely took the place of kin. A few wives said they went to the shops with another woman, or that they got errands for each other, or that they took turns at fetching the children from school. The more usual reaction was like that of Mrs Todd, who complained, 'When the baby was ill, not a soul knocked at my door to get me an errand.' Even where neighbours were willing to assist, people were apparently reluctant to depend on them too much or confide in them too freely. Mrs Hall, although she was helped by a neighbour at her recent confinement, said, 'I don't think you can go to a neighbour if you want anything personal.' Mrs Maggs said, 'If I'm ill she comes in and looks after the baby but it don't do to visit, does it?' 'My husband,' said Mrs Young, 'doesn't think it right to have neighbours in the place.'

LACK OF PLACES TO GO

One reason people have so little to do with neighbours is the absence of places to meet them. In Bethnal Green there is one pub for every 400 people, and one shop for every 44 (or one for every 14 households). At Greenleigh there is one pub for 5,000 people, and one shop for 300. Some services are not there at all. Cinemas, for instance – the nearest one is at Barnhurst,[2] several miles away, so far that the fares are 6d. each way. 'Then on top of that there's the ice in the picture palace and a quarter of sweets – makes it half a quid before you're through.'

1. The comparison is complicated by the fact that only 12 of the 19 wives at Greenleigh actually had a mother alive when they were confined, compared with 36 out of the 44 wives in Bethnal Green. But this does not invalidate the main conclusion about help given by mothers and other relatives.

2. This, like Greenleigh, and for the same reason, is a fictitious name.

So at Greenleigh practically no one goes out at night, except the small number of hardy people who attend meetings at the 'community centre', and the adolescents who can find nothing to do on the estate and spend the evening in East London before catching the last tube back. All the others stay at home, and a good many of them watch the television. The spread of television sets at Greenleigh and Bethnal Green is shown in Table 15.

TABLE 15: Television at Bethnal Green and Greenleigh

	Bethnal Green		Greenleigh	
	1953	1955	1953	1955
Television sets per 100 households	21	32	39	65

The G.P.O. Radio and Accommodation Department kindly supplied this information.

Not only is there a bigger proportion of sets on the estate; the increase between 1953 and 1955 was at a faster rate at Greenleigh than Bethnal Green.

The growth of television compensates for the absence of amenities outside the home, and serves to support the family in its isolation. Instead of going out to the cinema or the pub, the family sits night by night around the magic screen in its place of honour in the parlour. In one household the parents and five children of all ages were paraded around it in a half circle at 9 p.m. when one of us called; the two-month-old baby was stationed in its pram in front of the set. The scene had the air of a strange ritual. The father said proudly:

'The tellie keeps the family together. None of us ever have to go out now.'

FINANCIAL PARTNERSHIP

The television set has to be paid for and kept in repair – new cathode tubes can be a heavy cost. And that is not all. Rents are higher, actually nearly three times as high on average as they used to be in Bethnal Green.[1] Fares are higher. The cost of an early morning return[2] to Bethnal Green rose by half between 1953 and 1955, despite the growing crush which prompted one man to say 'if we were animals the R.S.P.C.A. would lock up the tube for cruelty.' New furniture has to be bought – one couple were struggling to repay £100 spent on a bedroom suite, another £191 spent on furniture when they first moved out. The lure of hire purchase, and the pressure of the tallyman, is difficult to resist. The children are said to eat more[3] and shoes wear out more quickly with the long walks to school, shops, and station.

Confronted by higher expenses all round, people could not have managed at all unless they saved on something else. The main sacrifice was made by the husbands. They had to increase their housekeeping allowances as well as meet the extra fares and the like, and to do this they had, unless they were able to earn more by a great deal of overtime, to economize on other things which they used to spend their money on before they moved. Many of the husbands gave up drinking, a change made all the easier by the absence of pubs. 'I was a very heavy drinker before,' said Mr Minton. 'I'm a teetotaller now.' Others said the same:

'It's definitely changed my whole way of life living down here. I used to go out every Wednesday night to play darts, for instance, and the wife used to come round later on in the evening and have a couple of stouts. I used to spend about two or three pounds a week on it. The last time I had a drink was when I saw my brother about fi~e weeks ago.'

'Well, if you're going to put your children first, you can't spend your money on drinking and smoking.'

1. This comparison is derived from a special inquiry made with the cooperation of the housing officials of the Metropolitan Borough of Bethnal Green and the London County Council.

2. A name recently substituted, as a sign of the times, for 'workman's ticket'.

3. Contrary to the impression of one of the Bethnal Green informants who would not go to a housing estate because people did not know how to eat there – 'out there it's all kippers and curtains.'

Mr Maggs, although he had cut down, was not to be done out of his Friday drink.

'Say you're coming home on a Friday night and you say to yourself I'd fancy a pint tonight. Well, you can't get it. You have to come home instead and get yourself a cup of tea. The result is, of course, that I have it in Bethnal Green before I leave.'

The majority of men (twenty-six out of thirty-nine) said they had reduced their spending on drinking and smoking after going to the estate. Generally speaking, the money saved came into the home instead. 'In Bethnal Green,' said Mr Morrow, 'I had £3 for myself, here it's only fifteen bob. I used to go to the boozer every night. In Greenleigh it's different. What I used to give to the publican goes into the home.' His wife, when we interviewed her separately, confirmed what her husband said:

'Women on this estate think themselves lucky if they have £1 left on a Monday. Some are worse off than me because their husbands don't give them their proper wages. My husband has given up the beer since we moved and he doesn't go to football matches any more.'

We can see that husbands not only do more to aid their wives in emergencies; they also spend less on themselves and more on their families. When they watch the television instead of drinking beer in the pub, and weed the garden instead of going to a football match, the husbands of Greenleigh have taken a stage further the partnership mentioned in an earlier chapter as one of the characteristics of modern Bethnal Green. The 'home' and the family of marriage becomes the focus of a man's life, as of his wife's, far more completely than in the East End. 'You lose contact with parents and relations once you move out here,' said Mr Curtis. 'You seem to centre yourself more on the home. Everybody lives in a little world of their own.'

We have in this chapter, to conclude, given a sketch of what happens when people move to the housing estate. We have discussed in turn the two sides of what is really a single change. When they leave the East End the people also leave their relatives behind them, and, although few of them cut the threads which connect them to their former homes, they can no longer see their old companions every day or even every week. In emergency, they can no longer so easily send word round to Mum's. When they arrive at Greenleigh, being deprived of relatives, they have to make do as best they can, sometimes with the aid of neighbours, but usually by their own devices. Children do more. Husbands do more. The family is more self-contained in bad times and in good.

Greenleigh, like anywhere else, has advantages as well as disadvantages, and, as always, human adaptability shows its power to find a compensation. There is the pleasure of washing baby in a bath with running hot water instead of a tub filled from kettles. There is the delight of a flower-garden on a hot summer's evening. There is the pride of showing the relatives the cupboards in the kitchen and the back-boiler which heats water as it heats space. There is variety and football on the tellie. There is the satisfaction of knowing that, even if they are making a sacrifice, it is for the good of their children, who are growing up in the country and attending fine schools which are the only public buildings on which money and ingenuity have been lavished. There is, above all, the possibility, even inside their own little home, of making good some of the loss of social life. Husband and wife are together and a closer partnership here can make isolation bearable. He is now the one who leads the active life of society, not only on the job but, sometimes too, on his round of the relatives after work is done. He is the messenger who brings back to Cambridge Avenue the news from the larger world of work and the smaller world of kinship. She is more dependent on him, for news and for the financial sacrifice which will sustain their domestic economy. If, now that he does not have to share her with so many others, he plays well his roles of messenger, earner, and companion, the strains of the new life are not without compensation.

10

KEEPING THEMSELVES TO
THEMSELVES

WE have now described some of the effects of migration.
People's relatives are no longer neighbours sharing the in-
timacies of daily life. Their new neighbours are strangers,
drawn from every part of the East End, and they are, as we
have seen, treated with reserve. In point of services, neighbours do not make up for kin.

Our informants were so eager to talk about their neighbours and generally about their attitude to other residents
on the estate, that we feel bound to report them. They frequently complained of the unfriendliness of the place, which
they found all the more mysterious because it was so different
from Bethnal Green. Why should Greenleigh be considered
unfriendly? This chapter tries to explain.

The prevailing attitude is expressed by Mr Morrow. 'You
can't get away from it, they're not so friendly down here.
It's not "Hello, Joe," "Hello, mate." They pass you with
a side-glance as though they don't know you.' And by Mr
Adams. 'We all come from the slums, not Park Lane, but
they don't mix. In Bethnal Green you always used to have
a little laugh on the doorstep. There's none of that in Greenleigh. You're English, but you feel like a foreigner here, I
don't know why. Up there you'd lived for years, and you
knew how to deal with the people there. People here are
different.' And by Mr Prince. 'The neighbours round here
are very quiet. They all keep themselves to themselves. They
all come from the East End but they all seem to change when
they come down here.'

Of the forty-one couples, twenty-three considered that
other people were unfriendly, eight were undecided one way
or another, and ten considered them friendly: the recorded
opinions are those of the couples, because in no interview

did husband and wife appear to hold strongly different views. How does this majority who consider their fellow residents unfriendly feel about themselves? Do they also label themselves unfriendly? No one admits it, some indignantly deny it. If they are hostile themselves, they do not acknowledge it, but attribute the feeling to others. Yet they mostly reveal that their own behaviour is the same as they resent in others; that (since *others* are unfriendly) to withdraw will avoid trouble and keep the peace; that co-existence is safer, because more realistic, than cooperation. 'The policy here is don't have a lot to do with each other, then there won't be any trouble,' says Mr Chortle succinctly.

This attitude is supported by reference to the skirmishes and back-biting which have resulted from being 'too friendly' in the past. 'It's better if you just talk to neighbours and don't get too friendly,' concludes Mr Sandeman from his past experience. 'You stop friends if you don't get to know them too well. When you get to know them you're always getting little troubles breaking out. I've had too much of that and so I'm not getting too friendly now.'

Mr Young told his wife – 'When I walk into these four walls, I always tell her "Don't make too many friends. They turn out to be enemies."' And one experience had turned Mr Yule into a recluse. 'We don't mix very well in this part of the estate. At first I used to lend every Tom, Dick, or Harry all my tools or lawn mower or anything. Then I had £20 pinched from my wallet. Now we don't want to know anyone – we keep ourselves to ourselves. There's a good old saying – the Englishman's home is his castle. It's very true.'

Usually the troubles are shadowy affairs which have happened to people other than oneself. 'We're friendly,' says Mr Wild in the usual style, 'but we don't get too involved, because we've found that causes gossip and trouble. We've seen it happen with other people, so we don't want it to happen to us. Now we keep ourselves to ourselves.' Whatever the justification, the result is the same. People do not treat others either as enemies or as friends.[1] They are wary, though polite. They pass the time of day in the road. They have an occasional word over the fence or a chat at the garden gate. They nod to each other in the shops. Neighbours even borrow and lend little things to each other, and when this accommodation is refused, it is a sign that acquaintance has turned into enmity. Mrs Chortle has broken off trading as well as diplomatic relations with one of her neighbours. 'These people are very dirty,' she said, 'and I've told them I don't want to borrow or lend.' So has Mrs Morrow, for the different reason that 'Just because they've got a couple of ha'pence more than you they don't want to know you. In Bethnal Green it was different – neighbours were more friendly.'

Even where relations have not been severed, there is little of the mateyness so characteristic of Bethnal Green. Mr Stirling summed it up by remarking – 'I don't mind saying hello to any of them, or passing the time of day with them, but if they don't want to have anything to do with me, I don't want to have anything to do with them. I'm not bothered about them. I'm only interested in my own little family. My wife and my two children – they're the people that I care about. My life down here is my home.'

Women feel the lack of friends, as of kin, more keenly than their menfolk. Those who do not follow their husbands into the society of the workplace – and loneliness is one of the common reasons for doing so – have to spend their day alone, 'looking at ourselves all day,' as they say. In one interview the husband was congratulating himself on having a house, a garden, a bathroom, and a TV – 'the tellie is a bit of a friend down here' – when his wife broke in to say,

1. The same thing has been noticed in other estates. Near Liverpool, for instance, 'The main issue for most people was, however, the importance of maintaining a distinction between a friend and an acquaintance, and of keeping neighbourly relationship within the bounds of acquaintanceship . . . "It's bad policy to make friends on the estate because sooner or later you fall out with them and that creates unpleasantness."' Mitchell, G. D. and Lupton, T. 'The Liverpool Estate', p. 70.

'It's all right for you. What about all the time I have to spend here on my own?' This difference in their life may cause sharp contention, especially in the early years.[1] 'When we first came,' said Mrs Haddon, 'I'd just had the baby and it was all a misery, not knowing anyone. I sat on the stairs and cried my eyes out. For the first two years we were swaying whether to go back. I wanted to and my husband didn't. We used to have terrible arguments about it. I used to say "It's all right for you. I have to sit here all day. You do get a break."'

Not that all women resent it. A few, like Mrs Painswick, actually welcome seclusion. She had been more averse to the quarrels amongst the 'rowdy, shouty' Bethnal Greeners than appreciative of the mateyness to which quarrels are the counterpart, and finds the less intense life of Greenleigh a pleasant contrast. 'In London people had more squabbles. We haven't seen neighbours out here having words.'

ABSENCE OF KIN

When people regard others as unfriendly, the comparisons they implicitly make are with Bethnal Green. We have already (in Chapter 7) discussed the reasons why people living in the borough considered that a friendly place. They and their relatives had lived there a long time, and consequently had around them a host of long-standing friends and acquaintances. At Greenleigh they neither share long residence with their fellow tenants nor as a rule have kin to serve as bridges between the family and the wider community. These two vital interlocked conditions of friendliness are missing, and their absence goes far to explain the attitude we have illustrated.

It also accounts for the astringency of the criticism. Migrants, whether to the United States or to housing

1. The shock effect of arrival has been noted in other surveys of housing estates. Thus the vicar of Watling commented: 'The loneliness of the people here in the first months after their removal to Watling is extreme. The women are mostly affected by that desperate loneliness.' Durant, R. op. cit., p. 60.

estates, always take part of their homeland with them, our informants like everyone else. They take with them the standards of Bethnal Green, derived from a close community of kindred and neighbours. Friends, within and without the kinship network, were the unavoidable accompaniment of the kind of life they led – too much so for devotees of quiet and privacy. They grew up with their friends, they met them at auntie's, for ten years they walked down the street with them to work. They are used to friendliness, and, their standards in this regard being so high, they are all the more censorious about the other tenants of the County Council. They are harsh in their comment, where someone arriving from a less settled district, or from another and even newer housing estate, might be accustomed to the standoffishness, and, by his canons, even impressed by the good behaviour, of the same neighbours.

It would not matter quite so much people being new-comers if they had moved into an established community. The place would then already have been criss-crossed with ties of kinship and friendship, and one friend made would have been an introduction to several. But Greenleigh was built in the late 1940s on ground that had been open fields before. The nearest substantial settlement, a few miles away at Barnhurst, is the antithesis of East London, an outer suburb of privately-owned houses, mainly built between the wars for the rising middle classes of the time. The distance between the estate and its neighbour is magnified by the resentment, real and imagined, of the old residents of Barn-hurst at the intrusion of rough East Enders into the rides of Essex and, what is worse, living in houses not very unlike their own put up at the expense of the taxpayer. 'People at Barnhurst look down on us. They treat us like dirt. They're a different class of people. They've got money.' 'It's not so easy for the girls to get boys down here. If people from the estate go to the dance hall at Barnhurst they all look down on them. There's a lot of class distinction down here.' These, the kind of thoughts harboured by the ex-Bethnal Greeners, do nothing to make for ease of communication between the two places. So there is no tradition into which the newcomers can enter. If Barnhurst has any influence upon Greenleigh, it is to sharpen the resentment of the estate against its environment and to stimulate the aspiration for material standards as high.

Nor would it matter quite so much if the residents of Greenleigh all had the same origin. No doubt if they all came from Bethnal Green, they would get on much better than they do: many of them would have known each other before and, anyway, at least have a background in common. As it is, they arrive from all over London, though with East Enders predominant. Such a vast common origin might be enough to bind together a group of Cockneys in the Western Desert; Western Essex is too near for that. When all are from London, no one is from London: they are from one of the many districts into which the city is divided. What is then emphasized is far more their difference than their sameness. The native of Bethnal Green feels himself different from the native of Stepney or Hackney. One of our informants, who had recently moved into Bethnal Green from Hackney, a few minutes away, told us 'I honestly don't like telling people I live in Bethnal Green. I come from Hackney myself, and when I was a child living in Hackney, my parents wouldn't let me come to Bethnal Green. I thought it was something terrible.' These distinctions are carried over to Greenleigh, where it is no virtue in a neighbour to have come from Stepney, rather the opposite. Mr Abbot summed it up as follows: 'You've not grown up with them. They come from different neighbourhoods, they're different sorts of people, and they don't mix.'

We had expected that, despite these disadvantages, people would, in the course of time, settle down and make new friendships, and our surprise was that this had not happened to a greater extent. The informants who had been on the estate longest had no higher opinion than others of the friendliness of their fellows. Four of the eighteen couples who had been there six or seven years judged other people to be friendly, as did six of the twenty-three couples with residence for five years or less. Mr Wild was one who commented on how long it was taking for time its wonders to perform.

'They're all Londoners here but they get highbrow when they get here. They're not so friendly. Coming from a turning like the one where we lived, we knew everyone. We were bred and born amongst them, like one big family we were. We knew all their troubles and everything. Here they are all total strangers to each other and so they are all wary of each other. It's a question of time, I suppose. But we've been here four years and I don't see any change yet. It does seem to be taking a very long while to get friendly.'

One reason it is taking so long is that the estate is so strung out – the number of people per acre at Greenleigh being only one-fifth what it is in Bethnal Green – and low density does not encourage sociability.

In Bethnal Green your pub, and your shop, is a 'local'. There people meet their neighbours. At Greenleigh they are put off by the distance. They don't go to the pub because it may take twenty minutes to walk, instead of one minute as in Bethnal Green. They don't go to the shops, which are grouped into specialized centres instead of being scattered in converted houses through the ordinary streets,[1] more than they have to, again because of the distance. And they don't go so much to either because when they get there, the people are gathered from the corners of the estate, instead of being neighbours with whom they already have a point of contact. The pubs and shops of Bethnal Green serve so well as 'neighbourhood centres' because there are so many of them: they provide the same small face-to-face groups with continual opportunities to meet. Where they are few and large, as at Greenleigh, they do not serve this purpose so well.

FROM PEOPLE TO HOUSE

The relatives of Bethnal Green have not, therefore, been

1. Out of the 1,214 shops in Bethnal Green in 1955, 766 had living accommodation attached to them, and only 458 were of the lock-up type of Greenleigh.

replaced by the neighbours of Greenleigh. The newcomers are surrounded by strangers instead of kin. Their lives outside the family are no longer centred on people; their lives are centred on the house. This change from a people-centred to a house-centred existence is one of the fundamental changes resulting from the migration. It goes some way to explain the competition for status which is in itself the result of isolation from kin and the cause of estrangement from neighbours, the reason why co-existence, instead of being just a state of neutrality – a tacit agreement to live and let live – is frequently infused with so much bitterness.

When we asked what in their view had made people change since they moved from East London, time and time again our informants gave the same kind of suggestive answers that people had become, as they put it, 'toffee-nosed', 'big headed', 'high and mighty', 'jealous', 'a cut above everybody else'.

'It's like a strange land in your own country,' said Mrs Ames. 'People are jealous out here. They're made to be much quieter in a high-class way, if you know what I mean. They get snobbish, and when you get snobbish you're not sociable any more.'

'I'm surprised,' said Mr Tonks 'at the way people vote Conservative at Greenleigh when the L.C.C. built these houses for them. One has a little car or something and so he thinks himself superior. People seem to think only of themselves when they get here.'

'The neighbour runs away with the idea that she's a cut above everybody else, but when you get down to brass tacks,' which Mrs Berry proceeded to do, 'she's worse off than you'll ever be. She's one of those people, you know what I mean, she's very toffee-nosed. There are some people down here who get like that.'

What about the informants themselves? Did they too think themselves superior? Just as people were less ready to label themselves 'unfriendly' than they were others, so they were less ready to admit they themselves felt superior. Not many showed their mind so clearly as Mrs Abbot who said, 'As soon as they get down here they get big ideas, and yet they've never been used to it. They're *nothing* really.' Or as

Mr Haddon – 'Some people are inclined to think they're better than some other people in the East End of London, but they're not. I've met them and mixed with them and I find that they're actually lower than the others – they haven't the ability to be sociable. That's what it is. So they put themselves a bit above others so as to give a let-out to their feelings.' Yet we formed the strong impression that most of the critics of the 'big-heads' did at least in part share the attitude they complained of.

One key to this attitude, as we have said, is the house. When they compare it with the gloomy tenement or decaying cottage, is it any wonder that they should feel they have moved up in the world?

'When people moved out here it was a big change for them,' said Mr Adams. 'In Bethnal Green the people were cooped up in two rooms or something like that, and when they get here they think they've bettered themselves – and so they have bettered themselves. And they try to raise their standard of living.'

A house is one bearer of status in any society – it most certainly is in a country where a semi-detached suburban house with a garden has become the signal mark of the middle classes. When the migrants compare the new with the old, is it any wonder that they should for a time feel 'big-headed'? In their mind's eye the people with whom they compare themselves may be less their fellow-residents at Greenleigh with their identical houses than their old neighbours of Bethnal Green, and, compared to them, they are in this one way undeniably superior.

Mr Berry, a milkman, was one of several who connected the 'snobbishness' with the possession of a new house.

'I deliver milk all over the estate so I think I know practically everybody on this estate. And I can tell you that when they move down here – I suppose it's just that they've got a new house – they just think they're a cut above everybody else.'

Mrs Allen, although rather more tentative, was of the same mind.

'I don't like it, the atmosphere. People are not the same; I don't know if they get big-headed because they've got a house. Out here you just get a good morning.'

The women most appreciate their new workshop and nursery. The man's status is the status of his job; the woman's the status of her home. Since she has moved up most in the world, she is only being realistic to recognize it.[1]

'When I was in London I had a four-roomed house on my own, but you get a few of them who come from, say, two rooms. Then they get a house. Well, they've worked hard – you must admit they've worked hard – they've got themselves a nice home, television, and all that. So you find this type of person temporarily gets a bit to thinking that they are somebody. You do find it with some people, and I think you find it more amongst the women than amongst the men.'

CHALLENGE OF A STYLE OF LIFE

The house when the builders leave it is only a shell. The house when people move into it comes to life. They bestow an authority upon it, even vest it with a kind of personality: up to a point it then decrees what they shall do within its walls. The house is also a challenge, demanding that their style of life shall accord with the standard it sets. When they make a first cup of tea after the removal van has driven away and look around their mansion, they are conscious not only of all they have got which they never had before but also of all the things they need which they still lack. The furniture brought from Bethnal Green looks old and forlorn against the bright paint. They need carpets for the lounge, lino for the stairs, and mats for the front door. They need curtains. They need another bed. They need a kitchen table. They need new lampshades, pots and pans, grass seed and

1. Compare what was said in the Liverpool inquiry. 'A tendency for them [wives] to be more status conscious than their husbands was observed, this being particularly true of the wives of skilled workers ... Women also attached more importance to symbols of superior status such as the television mast, the outward appearance of respectability and the need to "keep up with the Jones's".' Mitchell, G. D. and Lupton, T. op. cit., p. 49.

spades, clothes lines and bath mats, Airwick and Jeyes, mops and pails – all the paraphernalia of modern life for a house two or three times larger and a hundred times grander than the one they left behind them. With the aid of their belongings, they need somehow to live the kind of life, be the kind of people, that will fit into Forest Close or Cambridge Avenue. Then they, and the house, can at last be comfortable. They have to acquire new property. They have to acquire new habits. If they are to settle at Greenleigh, they have to make a profound adjustment in their lives: that is the challenge.

The first essential is money for material possessions. When people move to Greenleigh the standard of life, measured by the quality of housing, is at once raised. They attempt to bring the level in other respects up to the same standard. Furniture and carpets have to be bought, and although, with the aid of the ever more ubiquitous hire purchase, this can be done without capital, it cannot be done without a burden on income. Moreover, the house is only the beginning. A nice house and shabby clothes, a neat garden and an old box of a pram, do not go together. 'My sister gave me a beautiful Dunkley pram,' said Mrs Berry, 'because I was going to such a beautiful new house.' Smartness calls for smartness.

As well as appurtenances for the house, there is more need too for the sort of possessions which will improve communications with the outer world. The Bethnal Greener's society is close by. He does not need a telephone to make appointments to see his friends because they are only a few minutes away. He does not need a highly developed time-sense (as we discovered to our cost when interviewing) because it does not matter greatly whether he goes round to Mum's at 10 o'clock or 11. If Mum is not there someone will explain where she has gone. He does not have to have a car or a motor cycle because relatives and friends, even work, are at walking distance.

At Greenleigh a person has to organize his life more closely, develop a more exact sense of time, and be prepared to travel to avoid being cut off from social contact alto-gether.[1] In some ways the more self-contained home is less self-contained than ever. Greenleigh is part of a larger world. A person's shops are a mile off, his work six miles away, and his relatives ten or twenty miles away, some of them on the suburban circuit of housing estates – Oxhey, Debden, Harold Hill, Becontree – along which no buses ply. Distances to shops, work, and relatives are not walking distances any more. They are motoring distances: a car, like a telephone, can overcome geography and organize a more scattered life into a manageable whole. With a car he can, without having to expose himself to the wintry winds which blow over the fields, get to work, to his relatives in Bethnal Green Road, or to his friends who have gone over to Kent. 'Now that we've got the car,' said Mr Marsh, 'we can see the wife's sister at Laindon more often.' She was now seen every fortnight instead of every three or four months. Cars are beginning to move from luxury to neces-sity. 'I don't want to win £75,000. I just want to win £500 – so that I can get myself a little car. I could get a nice little car for that. You really need a car down here,' said Mr Adams. One of the more fortunate, Mr Berry, who had already achieved the two accomplishments of the complete man, discoursed on their necessity.

'There are two things that I think are essential when you live on an estate. One's a telephone, the other's a car. I don't like having to pay my telephone bill, but I think it's worth it. It means my brother can ring me up on the estate any time he wants to. And if you're in any trouble – if there's anything wrong with one of the boys say – I can ring up a doctor if I need one. You don't need a

1. The chief psychiatrist at a local hospital told us that the loneliness of the women on this and other housing estates was the immediate, precipitating cause of so many of them coming to his department for treatment. We were able to see his records but decided that it was not possible, with our lack of resources and medical knowledge, to check his statement with any meaningful quantitative data. The problem was, without visiting a very large number of psychiatric departments and mental hospitals, to get any significant comparative facts for the East End.

telephone in Bethnal Green, because the doctor's on the doorstep. Practically anywhere you live in Bethnal Green there's a doctor near at hand. And you need a car for travelling about. We're so far away from everywhere out here that it's actually cheaper to run a car than it is to pay fares.'

Greenleigh already has many more telephones than Bethnal Green, where you can go down the street to your relatives as quickly as, and more cheaply than, you can phone them; the figures for residential subscribers are eighty-eight per thousand at Greenleigh and only thirteen in Bethnal Green.

Greenleigh, though composed mainly of manual workers like Bethnal Green, has nearly seven times more telephones per head and, if our informants are any guide, at least one motive is to keep in touch with the kin left behind. 'We can't get up to see them very often,' said Mrs Adams. 'That's really why we had the phone put in here. If you can only hear each other it's something. It does keep you in touch with home.' But if telephones can be installed easily enough, garages cannot. They were not a necessity when the architects made the future in County Hall. A garage, now as rare in twentieth-century Greenleigh as an indoor lavatory was in nineteenth-century Bethnal Green, could be as much a motive for migration in the future. Cars, telephones, telegrams, and letters represent not so much a new and higher standard of life as a means of clinging to something of the old. Where you could walk to your enjoyment, you did not need a car. Where you cannot walk, and public transport is inconvenient or too expensive, you need a car.

This understandable urge to acquisition can easily become competitive. People struggle to raise their all-round standards to those of the home, and in the course of doing so, they look for guidance to their neighbours. To begin with, the first-comers have to make their own way. The later arrivals have their model at hand. The neighbours have put up nice curtains. Have we? They have got their garden planted with privet and new grass-seed. Have we?

159

They have a lawn-mower and a Dunkley pram. What have we got? The new arrivals watch the first-comers, and the first-comers watch the new arrivals. All being under the same pressure for material advance, they naturally mark each other's progress. Those who make the most progress are those who have proved their claim to respectability, Greenleigh-style. The fact that people are watching their neighbours and their neighbours watching them provides the further stimulus, reinforcing the process set in motion by the new house, to conform to the norms of the estate. There is anxiety lest they do not fit.

'People are not very friendly here. It's the same on all the estates. They've nothing else to do when they've finished work except watch you. It's all jealousy. They're afraid you'll get a penny more than they have. In London people have other things to occupy their minds. Here when they've done their work they've nothing to do. They're at the window and they notice everything. They say "Mrs Brown's got a new hat on." They don't miss anything. I think the trouble is they've never been used to a nice house. When they come from London they think they're high and mighty. If you've got something they'll go into debt to get it themselves.'

After the house has schooled its tenants, there is still much uncertainty about the proper way to behave in this new and strange environment. What the house does not do, the neighbours finish off. By their example they indicate the code to be followed. Hence, if one person has a refrigerator, next-door thinks she should have one; if A has a car, B wants one too.

'If,' says Mrs Abbot, 'you make your garden one way, they'll knock all theirs to pieces to make theirs like it. It's the same with curtains – if you put up new curtains, they have new curtains in a couple of months. And if someone buys a new rug they have to hang it on the line so you can see it.'

The struggle for possessions is one in which comparisons with other people are constantly made. Some of those who have achieved a more complete respectability look down on the others; those with less money resent the more successful and keep as far away from them as they can. 'The whole answer is – the whole trouble is, many men can't earn enough. They have to hide behind curtains. They've got a certain amount of pride.' Resentment may also produce an aggressive spirit. 'This place is all right for middle-class people, people with a bit of money. It's no good for poorer people – I think they've all got money troubles, that's why they're so spiteful to each other.'

We have been arguing that, the possession of a new house having sharpened the desire for other material goods, the striving for them becomes a competitive affair. The house is a major part of the explanation. But there is more to it than that.

KINSHIP AND STATUS

In Bethnal Green people, as we said earlier, commonly belong to a close network of personal relationships. They know intimately dozens of other local people living near at hand, their school-friends, their work-mates, their pub-friends, and above all their relatives. They know them well because they have known them over a long period of time. Common family residence since childhood is the matrix of friendship. In this situation, Bethnal Greeners are not, as we see it, concerned to any marked extent with what is usually thought of as 'status'. It is true, of course, that people have different incomes, different kinds of jobs, different kinds of houses – in this respect there is much less uniformity than at Greenleigh – even different standards of education. But these attributes are not so important in evaluating others. It is personal characteristics which matter. The first thing they think of about Bert is not that he has a 'fridge' and a car. They see him as bad-tempered, or a real good sport, or the man with a way with women, or one of the best boxers of the Repton Club, or the person who got married to Ada last year. In a community of long-standing, status, in so far as it is determined by job and income and education, is more or less irrelevant to a person's worth. He is judged instead, if he is judged at all, more in the round, as a person with the usual mixture of all kinds of qualities, some good, some bad, many indefinable. He is more of a life-portrait than a figure on a scale.

People in Bethnal Green are less concerned with 'getting on'. Naturally they want to have more money and a better education for their children.[1] The borough belongs to the same society as the estate, one in which standards and aspirations are moving upwards together. But the urge is less compulsive. They stand well with plenty of other people whether or not they have net curtains and a fine pram. Their credit with others does not depend so much on their 'success' as on the subtleties of behaviour in their many face-to-face relationships. They have the security of belonging to a series of small and overlapping groups, and from their fellows they get the respect they need.

How different is Greenleigh we have already seen. Where nearly everyone is a stranger, there is no means of uncovering personality. People cannot be judged by their personal characteristics: a person can certainly see that his neighbour works in his back garden in his shirt sleeves and his wife goes down to the shops in a blue coat, with two canvas bags: but that is not much of a guide to character. Judgement must therefore rest on the trappings of the man rather than on the man himself. If people have nothing else to go by, they judge from his appearance, his house, or even his Minimotor. He is evaluated accordingly. Once the accepted standards are few, and mostly to do with wealth, they become the standards by which 'status' is judged. In Bethnal Green it is not easy to give a man a single status, because he has so many; he has, in addition to the status of citizen, a low status as a scholar, high as a darts-player, low as a bargainer, and high as a story-teller. In Greenleigh, he has something much more nearly approaching one status because

1. The proportion of people saying they wanted a grammar-school education for their children was indeed no less in Bethnal Green than at Greenleigh. How far this was because there are more grammar-school places available for Bethnal Green children than in Essex, where the population has grown so much, we do not know.

something much more nearly approaching one criterion is used: his possessions.

Or rather we should say that the family has one status. The small group which lives inside the same house hangs together, and where people are known as 'from No. 22' or '37', their identity being traced to the house which is the fixed entity, each one of them affects the credit of the other. The children, in particular, must be well dressed so that neighbours, and even more school-friends and teachers, will think well of them, and of the parents.

'We always see that the children look smart. At these new schools, you like them to go to school respectable. We like to keep them up to the standard out here.'

The status is that of the family of marriage much more sharply than it is in Bethnal Green. In Bethnal Green the number of relatives who influence a person's standing is much larger, and they also are varied in their attributes. From a prominent local personality, a street-trader, say, a councillor, or a publican, a person can borrow prestige; but through another relative he may be associated with a less enviable reputation. One connexion confers high status, another low. It is therefore all the more difficult to give a person a single rating. On the other hand, the comparative isolation of the family at Greenleigh encourages the kind of simplified judgement of which we have been speaking.

People at Greenleigh want to get on in the light of these simple standards, and they are liable to be more anxious about it just because they no longer belong to small local groups. Their relationships are window-to-window, not face-to-face. Their need for respect is just as strong as it ever was, but instead of being able to find satisfaction in actual living relationships, through the personal respect that accompanies almost any steady human interaction, they have to turn to the other kind of respect which is awarded, by some strange sort of common understanding, for the quantity and quality of possessions with which the person surrounds himself. Those are the rules of the game and they are, under strong pressure from the neighbours, almost universally observed. Indeed, one of the most striking things about Greenleigh is the great influence the neighbours have, all the greater because they are anonymous. Though people stay in their houses, they do in a sense belong to a strong and compelling group. They do not know their judge personally but her influence is continuously felt. One might even suggest, to generalize, that the less the personal respect received in small group relationships, the greater is the striving for the kind of impersonal respect embodied in a status judgement. The lonely man, fearing he is looked down on, becomes the acquisitive man; possession the balm of anxiety; anxiety the spur to unfriendliness.

We took as the starting point of this chapter people's remarks, so frequent and vehement as to demand discussion, about the unfriendliness of their fellow residents. We have suggested two main explanations. Negatively, people are without the old relatives. Positively, they have a new house. In a life now house-centred instead of kinship-centred, competition for status takes the form of a struggle for material acquisition. In the absence of small groups which join one family to another, in the absence of strong personal associations which extend from one household to another, people think that they are judged, and judge others, by the material standards which are the outward and visible mark of respectability.

*

With this chapter we conclude our brief account of the estate. One obvious question will occur to the reader. Is what is happening now only temporary? Before we leave the subject it may therefore be worth speculating for a moment about the future. In the report as a whole we have laid a good deal of emphasis on length of residence. The difference between the two places which have figured in the inquiry can be attributed in part to time: in one place, but not in the other, people have lived long enough to put down roots. Is the implication that, as the years pass and the newness wears off the bricks and the people, Greenleigh will become more like Bethnal Green? Is time on the side of kinship? When the children of today grow into the mothers and fathers of tomorrow, will the three generations again form family clusters? After all, Bethnal Green was once a Greenleigh.

If the children *do* stay, then history will do what it has a habit of doing. Mrs Yule is now thirty. By the time she is sixty-five her four children may well be married with children of their own. If they live at Greenleigh, Mrs Yule, like her mother before her, will be a 'Mum' surrounded by her children and grandchildren. The decision partly rests with the children. Will they wish to stay on the estate? They are growing up there. Many of the parents still talk of Bethnal Green as 'up home'. Not so the children. To them, if they were small when they came, Bethnal Green is already a strange place, far off in the legendary East End.

'When we go back to Bethnal Green – to see the relations – the children hang about and say "Come on Mum, when are we going home." '

'Sometimes we ask the children to torment them if they'll go back to London.'

If we are right that length of residence creates territorial attachment, then one might expect these children to be as chary of departing from Greenleigh as their parents were from Bethnal Green. The localized kinship network would spread out again.

But today's children are growing up with their own ideas. Our time has its own values, perhaps prizing more the individual and less the group, whether of family or any other kind. To grow up may mean increasingly to grow away. The virtues of movement, from one area to another, from one job to another, from one set of beliefs to another, may be stressed more than the virtues of stability, tradition, and community, and where the new is praised and the old reproved, perhaps the strength of the time-spanning family is bound to be less than in a more steady state. The kinship patterns of the future may then be different from those we have described, as much in harmony with the new society as their forerunners were with the old. These are subtle influences, stemming from different conditions of life and continually re-crystallized in new sets of value-judgements. They will affect (though we do not know how) the whole society of which the housing estate, if bulking steadily larger in relative importance, is only a part. On this continuum Greenleigh and Bethnal Green are both moving.

Even if the younger generation want to stay, whether they can will not depend upon them alone any more than it did upon their parents alone. The physical environment may again limit their choice. If, in particular, there are no jobs and no houses, they will have to migrate once more. About jobs we can forecast with some certainty. A trading estate of new factories is being built now; ten or twenty years on there should be plenty of local jobs, though not necessarily those the children want to take. About houses we cannot be so sure. We can already see that special difficulties are likely to flow from the peculiar age structure of the population.

Youth predominates in new settlements from the frontier towns of Canada to the kibbutzim of Israel. The young are ready to move, the old less so. The general here applies to the particular with special force: the builders of the estates have reinforced self-selection by deliberate policy. From a short-term point of view this is all very understandable: families with young children are in the greatest need; the new estates should be built for them. But in the long run the authorities, by thinking only of the present, are laying up the most perplexing problems for themselves and their tenants in the future. Just as trouble sets in when the ecological balance of a natural environment is altered, so do difficulties mount when the age structure of a population is upset.

Greenleigh is a case in point. Its present residents, mostly couples with young children, fall mainly into two age-groups, the parents between thirty and forty-five, and the children under fourteen. At present the 'bulge' of children is so large that their need for schools is greatly taxing the education authorities. In ten to twenty years time the bulge of children will have become a bulge of married couples. With schools emptier and homes crammed, the burden will be transferred from the education to the housing committee. The need for houses will be as great then as the need for schools is now. This can be shown from a special analysis we carried out of what is likely to happen to Greenleigh's population, and to the demand for houses, in the years up to 1985.

By 1970 many of the present children will be of marriage age. But where are they to live? We estimate that in the thirty years up to 1985 over 2,500 additional houses, at least a third more than there were in 1955, will be required for new married couples from the estate. Since there are no sites left for further building, we would forecast with some confidence that the necessary number of new houses will not be put up at Greenleigh, and if this is so, when they become adults, most of the children are going to have to migrate again.

Unless the London County Council changes its view, the married couples of tomorrow may not even be able to occupy such existing houses as are vacated by death or voluntary removal. The council's present policy is that outsiders should usually be given preference over children – houses falling vacant on the country estates being mainly for citizens from inside the county, the electors to whom the L.C.C. owes its first responsibility.

The ruling has not gone without challenge. Dagenham is the oldest of the L.C.C. country estates. When first opened in the 1920s, its age composition was not unlike that of Greenleigh today;[1] its present condition is some indication of Greenleigh's future. At the end of 1955 the Dagenham Housing Applicants' Association appealed to residents in all the eighteen out-county estates to join in protest on behalf of the children of tenants.

1. See Young, T. op. cit., pp. 115–16.

At Dagenham, following protests by the Dagenham Borough Council, an annual quota of L.C.C. houses had been allocated to the sons and daughters of tenants, but it was only a minority of those falling vacant each year; and the local council itself could not build the extra houses needed. Of the 4,400 applicants on the borough list, 3,000 had to be told at the end of 1954 that there was no hope of them ever being housed within the township. 'We are in opposition,' declared the Association at the end of 1955, 'to the view that people are simply units to be moved about the face of the earth in line with the impersonal schemes of some "Big Brother" ... Help us to surround the County Hall with such a ring of fire from all out-county estates that consciences will be aroused and permanent community freedom granted without delay to every one of them.'[1]

The council may eventually respond to the appeal. Yet even if it does, and allows more children to be near their parents, it will still be up against the unavoidable shortage of houses in the towns it has built. The method by which the council has eased the housing shortage in the middle of the century is bound to create a further shortage in its last quarter.

We can now see how fraught with consequence is the decision to move young couples out of the city. A district which comprises a stable population of all ages is able to go far towards meeting its own housing needs. Houses (though we may sometimes regret it) usually last for more than a lifetime, and grandchildren can take over the houses of grandparents (their own or someone else's) when they die. But once upset the age structure by moving out the children as a group, and the relation of population to housing is so much disturbed that further disruptions are almost inevitable later on. For purposes of housing, if for no other, a three-generation community has evident advantages. Once a two-generation structure is established, as at Greenleigh, it is likely to be perpetuated, not there but elsewhere, by requiring the married children to move again. So when the

1. Reported in *The Times*, 28 December 1955.

authorities decide to uproot today's children they are, since they will not be able to avoid responsibility for the outcome, committing themselves to uproot and rehouse tomorrow's children as well. They are ensuring that Greenleigh will not soon be able to grow into another Bethnal Green; that the tenants of tomorrow are unlikely to be bound to each other by the same ties that we observed in the borough.

11

MOVEMENT BETWEEN CLASSES

WHAT we found on the housing estate does not detract from the sharpness of the conclusion we reached in the borough: it rather confirms the influence of residence upon kinship. In the city, couples usually live close to their relatives, and particularly to the wife's parents. At Greenleigh the family is, by the standards of Bethnal Green, isolated not only from kin but, it appears, from fellow residents as well. A new residence, a new life.

And yet in thus stressing geography we were concerned lest we were overlooking a still more powerful influence. If we neglected 'social mobility', the movement from one occupational class to another, would we be ignoring something of even greater importance than geographical mobility? Force has been given to the question by some leading sociologists. Parsons attributed the 'structural isolation of the conjugal family' in the American middle classes to the peculiar character of the occupational system, which 're-quires scope for the valuation of personal achievement, for equality of opportunity, for mobility in response to technical requirements, for devotion to occupational goals and interests relatively unhampered by "personal" considerations'.[1] He rather suggests that people dedicated to occupational achievement cannot at the same time be devoted to their families of origin. In a recent English work, Glass, speaking of movement from one status to another, says that 'actual movement itself may, save in special circumstances, distort or destroy kinship associations, with possible personal and social deprivation'.[2] Before coming to our final conclusions it may, in view of these statements, be worthwhile to see

1. Parsons, T. 'The Kinship System of the Contemporary United States', p. 244.
2. Glass, D. V. Intro. to *Social Mobility in Britain*, p. 25.

whether the interviews can throw any light at all upon this question. Working-class quarter as it is, Bethnal Green is obviously not a good place in which to pursue this subject. People who change their class also move out of the East End. We cannot therefore benefit from the experience of our informants who were, at Greenleigh too, themselves nearly all manual workers. The best we could do in the ordinary interviews was to inquire about their relatives who had achieved this form of worldly success.

The couples in the marriage samples at Bethnal Green and Greenleigh had between them 554 full siblings aged twenty-one or over. The brothers can be assigned to one or other of the Registrar-General's social classes according to their occupations; and the sisters according to their husbands' occupations if married, or according to their own if not. Our informants were not sufficiently precise about the occupations of 86 siblings or their husbands, or about the place of residence of five, to enable them to be included. The five siblings with whom informants were living have also been excluded in order to avoid the necessity of attributing a notional contact to people seeing each other constantly. The following analysis is therefore confined to the 458 siblings for whom full particulars were given.

The degree to which our informants (nearly all of them were themselves manual workers) maintained contact with

TABLE 16: Contacts with Siblings of Different Social Classes

(Bethnal Green and Greenleigh marriage samples combined)

	Professional and clerical	Manual	Total
Number of siblings	56	402	458
Average contacts with each sibling per year	17	41	38

'Professional' and 'clerical' combine the Registrar-General's Classes I and II with the non-manual occupations in his Class III, and 'manual' the remainder of his Class III with his Classes IV and V.

their brothers and sisters in different social classes is shown in Table 16. The lower the social class of their siblings, the more people see of them. To judge by this evidence, difference in social class certainly acts as a barrier between relatives.

But this is not the full story. For siblings in the higher social classes also live further away. Some of them moved during the war and thereafter succeeded in getting a good job in another part of the country. Others secured jobs first and moved afterwards, either because the work was elsewhere or, more often, because they wanted, and could now afford to pay for, a better house than they could find in Bethnal Green. Unlike the people now at Greenleigh, they did not have to wait upon the local authorities. They could of their own accord rent or buy a house in a suburb inhabited by other 'middle-class' people of the type they mixed with at work. A brother who was an accountant, for example, lived in his own house at Ilford, a production manager at Northolt, a draughtsman in Finchley, an engineer in Harrow, a fire assessor in Toronto, a manager of a cannery in Grimsby. The East End does not provide 'middle-class' people with 'middle-class' places to live, and such migration may therefore be more common than it would be in districts with more of a mixture of classes. A similar inquiry undertaken in such an area might well yield different results, merely because siblings in higher classes did not live so far away.

The lesser contact with higher-class siblings is clearly due in part to distance. We attempted to discover how much effect it had by making a comparison with siblings in manual occupations who were also living at a distance, and found that our informants saw as little of them. Provided that both were living at the same distance, people saw about as much of their siblings in 'white-collar' as in manual jobs. This conclusion does not, of course, mean that class has no influence upon contact; it has a marked influence but one exerted mainly through the effect it has upon residence.

Most people did not suggest that the good fortune of their siblings had led to embarrassment. A few exceptional ones were affected not so much by the distance as by a more subtle element in the relationship. They referred to the strain between them. They thought that their brothers or sisters had somehow been changed, and for the worse, by their advancement: they put on airs, they were superior, they were standoffish. 'Since he's the manager he sort of knows it,' said Mr Flood.

They were especially blamed for avoiding their obligations to their parents and to 'the family': they had allowed their good jobs to override their duty to the kindred. Mrs Power, for example, said that:

'Dick is well-to-do. He owns an ice-cream business but he won't give any help to his Mum. His wife is stuck up. Her father is a sales manager for some big firm and she thinks she's better than Princess Margaret and she won't even set foot in the East End. They haven't been near Mum for years.'

Mr Jones made a similar complaint:

'Harry is the only one who never comes near to see his parents. He's got his own business at Fulham and has bought a big house and is too busy with the business to bother about us.'

Mr Florence coupled the stock criticism with the one that he had personally been treated badly as well.

'My sister's husband has got a big car and they live in a lovely house. They think themselves too good. When I last saw him John treated me like one of his staff. He knows I smoke but he wouldn't even offer me a cigarette. He's jumped himself up. They don't do anything for Dad any more.'

Two men have had a different experience, the parents having taken sides against them. Mr Madge's parents have moved to Wembley so as to live near one of their sons who had built up his own business there, and now they too are blamed: 'She never comes over here to see us, although she's got a nice car and everything.' Mr Lamb does not get on with his brother now that he is a manager.

173

'He's standoffish. He's bought his own house and he wouldn't help a soul. Money gets some of them, doesn't it?'

And since, despite the criticism, his mother has sided with his brother, he sees nothing of her either. His remarks, like the others we have quoted, are those of exceptional individuals. They merely illustrate the attitude of a few people for whom class makes a gulf greater than distance.

ASCENT THROUGH THE SCHOOL

Whatever these siblings did was by their own efforts, after their formal education was finished. Does ascent by the school have a different effect on the family? The question is pertinent because the post-war educational reforms, coupled with full employment, have given more manual workers' children the chance of going to grammar schools and getting non-manual jobs after they leave. If higher education modifies the kinship system, it is going to affect more working-class families than in the past.

In order to investigate the question at all we had to go to the grammar schools themselves for the names of ex-pupils. The various samples which served for other purposes were of no use for this. In the past so few Bethnal Green children enjoyed higher education that our samples contained hardly any of them. Only 4 per cent of the people of all ages in the general sample stayed at school until they were sixteen years old. We needed the names of people of approximately the same age, old enough and married for long enough so that if they were to break away from their families of origin they would have already done so. We finally obtained from two important local grammar schools, which were, as it happens, over the border in Stepney and Hackney, a list of all the 67 Bethnal Green girls who had completed the course in the five years immediately preceding the war; and from these we drew a sample of 40. No more than 24 of the girls, now grown-up, could be traced after the interval of nearly twenty years since they were at school and it took so long to do even this that we had no time for the boys' schools. Since (as explained more fully in the Appendix) the sample has other defects as well, the results have no statistical significance and they are only reported because on this question the other samples are of no help at all.

Our interest was in what had happened subsequently to the girls' relationship with their parents and other relatives. But to understand what *had* happened we needed to know something about the kinds of families they came from to begin with,[1] and that meant going back to the thirties, as far as memory could be a guide. Attendance at a grammar school was then extremely rare. A headmaster who had been in his post for twenty years told us how extraordinary it was, in the days when children were kept at home because they had no boots, for pupils from his elementary school to 'win the scholarship'. The names of the few scholars were inscribed in letters of gold on the small Honours Board at the school entrance. By now the wind has changed: the headmaster discussed the qualifying IQ level for admission to grammar schools as though it were an everyday matter. In the thirties his concern was hooliganism in the playground; in the fifties it is the 11+ exam. One of our informants was the first girl at another elementary school to pass the scholarship. On the great day she came into the house and in a casual way said, 'Mum, I've passed.' Then she broke down, and soon afterwards a messenger arrived from the headmistress to summon mother to the school to receive her congratulations and take part in the rejoicing of the staff. Her school was given a special half-holiday.

The pleasure of the teachers was not generally shared. It was a breach of custom for little women to go to secondary schools to prepare for paper work in offices, and, if they did,

1. A recent government report has called for inquiry into the home background of working-class children at grammar schools, so many of whom still leave before they have finished the course. 'It is most important that further research into the problem of the effect of the home background, particularly that of the semi-skilled and unskilled worker, upon a child's education at a grammar school should be undertaken ... ' *Early Leaving*, p. 35. It would certainly be interesting to compare current experience with our historical reconstruction.

175

they were made to feel their peculiarity. They lost the friends who had formerly been their classmates; there was probably no one else in the whole street going to the same grammar school. When they came home in the afternoon they were supposed to do homework instead of rushing into the street to play. They became different, lonely, 'sort of reserved', regarded as 'someone apart'. 'Oh, look at her,' the other girls shouted after one of them. The uniform was a special trial – a mark of superior status detested because it made them feel inferior. At one of the schools it was a gym tunic that 'stopped three inches above the knee', a panama hat in the summer and a black velour in the winter, gloves, and long black woollen stockings which the girls could change for flesh-coloured ones only when at last they reached an upper form.

'All the children in the street would laugh at me. "Rotten 'at" they shouted at me as I went by. I used to push the straw hat down to the bottom of my satchel, and twist it up as much as I could to hide it. I pulled my gym tunic down as much as possible over my legs. All the others went to an ordinary school and they didn't think much of us at all.'

'I felt an outcast in the street directly I started going to the new school. I used to pick the butcher's daughter up sometimes who went, but otherwise I was quite alone. I remember the gym tunic, how I hated it.'

'I was more or less ostracized by the other girls in the street. The other kids made fun of us secondary school girls. They would shout out something about being stuck up or "swank pot". It was not just that they made fun of us, we just didn't have much in common. They had different ideas and I had mine, going to a different school like that.'

Their non-conformity was again very apparent when they reached fourteen, then the minimum leaving age. All the other girls in the street left school and went to work at a proper manual job. Our informants did not. Unlike other girls of the same age, who were dressed up smartly 'with little gee-gaws in their ears', they had no money to spend on themselves.

'I do remember two girls who had just started work, and I used to pass them every day going to the bus stop. They wouldn't speak to me any more. They were probably thinking "the lazy little so and so".'

Adults were hardly more sympathetic, if less vocal, than the children. This was a working-class community, and those who tried to become something else were not behaving as they should. One of our Jewish informants explained the lack of interest in education.

'We were Jewish immigrants and so we had no class really. It was different for us. The English working class had a fear of being thought snobs. I can remember two girls who won scholarships but did not take them up and I am sure it was not on account of the money, they could have afforded it, but they thought it was above their station to go to grammar school.'

One of the mothers told us how strongly her husband's relatives felt about it. His family was united against the scholarship. It was not right, they said, because 'his family were a family of work-people. Some of them said I ought to be ashamed of myself.' But the mother stood her ground against all the attacks. 'I said, "she's going as far as she can go."'

There was another kind of class pressure at school. The pupils did not come only from the East End. Some of them travelled up every day from the suburbs, from Ilford and Woodford. Nurses brought some of the younger ones up and waited for them outside the gates in the afternoon. 'I remember there was a nurse in a thingummy for the Lamport children.' They were paid for, which was somehow better than having a scholarship. The uniforms at least made them look alike, and whenever they had parties they all had to come in fancy dress – a double disguise – so that the finery of the richer girls would not put the East Enders to shame. But 'the Ilford set' spoke differently and, although the Bethnal Green girls soon became bilingual (for they would have been as much criticized for speaking Cockney at school as they would for 'putting on airs' and speaking 'posh' at home), they were liable even so to feel awkward and inferior.

MOTHERS WERE KEENEST

Why did they do it? Why so unorthodox? The explanation lies with their families. They were in general supported by their parents, or at any rate by their mothers. Nine of the girls said their mothers were keener than their fathers that they should stay at school, five that both parents were keen, none that the father was keener. 'I went to the grammar school,' said one, 'because my mother was quite determined I should go there and stay there.' 'My mother was set,' said another, 'on my going there. I think it was the maternal instinct. They're ambitious for their brood.' One of the mothers put it in a slightly different way. 'I always wanted them to have a good start, having inflicted life on them. Mr Masters, well I don't want to run him down, but he didn't bother much.'

This does not answer but transforms the question: why were the parents, and especially the mothers, so unorthodox? Several of the Jewish ones, first-generation immigrants from Russia and Poland, were brought up in peasant villages where there were few schools. 'I mustn't grumble,' said one. 'I can read and write a little even though I never went to school.' They were determined that their children, the second-generation immigrants, should have the education of which they were deprived. As for the Gentiles, two of the mothers had been to grammar schools themselves, and wanted their daughters to do the same, and to get full advantage from it instead of the only partial benefit which they had got themselves: 'I wanted her to go all the way.' One father had built up a kind of legend about his own father who 'went to school' – that he went to school at all was a source of pride. 'He had to pay 3d. a week for it, to the School Board of London.' This family had a tradition of interest in education. But the main concern was security. The parents had suffered from unemployment, and they did not want their daughters to go through it too. 'He knew what unemployment was, long spells of it. He thought the school would give us a chance of a more secure job.' 'Her idea was that I stay on at school and be able to get a safe job at the end of it. She decided I was to go into the Civil Service, as it was a job with a pension at the end. That was her idea of heaven.'

There remain seven girls who said that neither of their parents had been keen on them going to grammar school, and three who did not know. They sat for the scholarship exam, and rather to the surprise, or chagrin, of their parents, they passed. 'I won it, that's all.' The parents, again especially the fathers, were not pleased to hear the news, but after the event they felt they should not 'stand in the way'.

Success for the daughters meant sacrifice for the parents. Nineteen of them received grants from the L.C.C., but these did little more than cover the expense of the uniforms, and all the parents had to forgo the earnings which the daughters would have brought into the home had they gone out to work at the usual age. Or rather the mothers had to. Then, as now, working children gave part of their earnings to their mother, not to their father; and since it was she who benefited in one event, so it was she who suffered in the other. Whether the mother was able to do without depended, more than anything else, upon the child's birth order. The younger children could go because by the time they arrived at the school-age there were already older children at work bringing money into the home. Three of the girls were only children, and the financial stringency was much less anyway in these families. Out of the other twenty-one, eleven of the girls were the youngest children, and eight were second youngest. The other two were the eldest, but in their families all of the children went to grammar school, in one because the father was a factory manager and could afford it, and in the other because the mother had a remarkably strong will and was determined that, whatever the sacrifice, all her very able children should get on. The girls themselves were as well aware as their sometimes resentful older

siblings of the importance of birth order.[1] As one sister
said:

'She was the youngest, the youngest of seven, and so by the time
she went to the grammar school there were the others of us to help
out. If it had been me I could never have gone. It wouldn't have
mattered if I'd won a scholarship or not. I just couldn't have gone.
When I was that age there were six of us to keep.'

Or as a mother put it:

'It was always that way with the oldest. With big families we
were waiting for them to go to work. The younger ones were better
off in every way. They got the best of the education and they got
the advantage of better jobs too.'

TWENTY YEARS LATER

These girls were, as we have said, extremely unusual people.
Only the support of their families enabled them to withstand the pressure of the community. Now we can consider
the effect which their education has had. The women (no
longer called girls, since we are talking about fifteen to
twenty years later) fall into three groups. First, the six
women who are single or separated from their husbands.
Second, the nine women who have married into a higher
social class – that is, whose husbands are of higher class than
their fathers. Third, the nine whose husbands are of the
same or of lower social class than their fathers.

All the women still single or separated are living at home
or working with their mothers. For them higher education
has not drawn them away from their parents; it may, indeed,
have done the opposite, by keeping them single. They themselves raised the question whether their chances of marriage
had been prejudiced. Two of them complained that, in a
district almost exclusively composed of manual workers with
no more than elementary education, they could not find

1. A post-war study of grammar-school boys showed that they
contained a very high proportion of *eldest* sons. Higher wages may have
affected the influence of birth order. Himmelweit, H. T. 'Social Status
and Secondary Education since the 1944 Act: Some Data for London',
pp. 145–6.

men with whom they had interests in common. Either the men thought them superior, or they thought the men narrow. One of them envied the women lucky enough to fail the scholarship exams.

'Education widens your outlook. It makes you dissatisfied. Look at all the other girls who were with me at my elementary school. They mostly got married pretty young and have settled down.'

Another was aware that most of the men were poor in Bethnal Green, and this was not what she wanted.

'I swore I would never marry anyone poor. I was determined to stay single for the rest of my life if necessary rather than do that.'

It has proved unnecessary. She has married a man at Finchley.

The husband's job seems to be decisive for the married majority. Nine of the women have married a husband in the same or in a lower social class than their parents. Their education does not seem to have made much difference either to their lives or to their relations with their families. As for the nine who have married upwards, their husbands are mainly in the professions – they number an accountant, an engineer, a librarian, a civil servant, an industrial chemist, a surveyor, a factory manager, a farmer, and a clerk. When we went from seeing the parents to their present homes, the contrast was as sharp as between Bethnal Green and Green-leigh, sometimes more so. Mrs Briggs, for instance, lives in an old block in one of the turnings off Bethnal Green Road; her daughter, now Mrs Cranford, is married to a surveyor living in his own house at Amersham. To reach the mother you go into an asphalt yard and climb a dark, winding flight of stone stairs; to reach the daughter you walk along a road bordered with gardens to a large bungalow with bow windows. The mother's living-room has faded brown wallpaper and is furnished with a sofa and two armchairs covered in shiny old rexine. The walls of the daughter's room are plain yellow, set off by a fitted blue carpet and a contemporary suite upholstered in red weave. One room looks out on to a shaft lined with dark grey walls descending to a court, the other has french windows opening on to beds of flowers. The mother has family photographs on the sideboard. Pride of place is given to a studio portrait of Mrs Cranford before her marriage, with her round pretty face, curly hair, necklace, and modish silk dress. The daughter has no photographs on show, only a small book-case full of bright Penguin books. The mother wears a greasy, shapeless overall, the daughter a smart black coat and skirt. The mother speaks strong Cockney; her daughter without a trace of it. The daughter talks of sending her son to a private boarding school as though it were taken for granted.

We travel from one house to another wondering what effect all this has had. Perhaps the most striking fact is that not one of the daughters who have married into the professions has broken off relations with her parents. They saw their mothers on average once a fortnight. This was much less than the daughters who had married manual workers, but the difference is once again partly due to distance. All except one of the former group live outside Bethnal Green, five in the suburbs of London, one in Gloucester, one in Southampton, and Mrs Cranford at Amersham. They live further away from their parents than the other women and for this reason alone they are bound to see them less. One of them said, 'I'm sure higher education does break up the family. It pushes you out geographically anyway. My mother used to envy the woman next door who had lots of children who visited her all the time with their children. But on the other hand my mother can sit back in comfort. We all contribute.' It is the same with the siblings. The women who have married upwards saw each of their brothers and sisters on average no more than twice a month; the other women saw each of them four times a week. The difference is accounted for in part by geography.

Migration is not the only effect of education. Most of the women know, for instance, that they speak 'better' than their parents, and they are anxious that their own children should speak better too. One of the women was upset be cause some of the neighbours' children in the suburban street where they lived had said to her daughter 'Wotcher Maureen'. Her mother tried to comfort her, while the interview was in progress, by explaining 'Well, that's just a phrase they're going through.' Her daughter did not seem to be convinced. They also recognize the difference in interests. 'In a way I think education can be a barrier. I think one has to be careful what one says. One might say something which was quite natural to oneself because of the education but they might think was put on. I think TV is making a lot of difference though. TV is a sort of god. They take it in in a flash. Whereas if I told them they wouldn't believe it.' They recognize, however well they manage themselves, that their husbands, and even more their friends, do not fit in with their parents. Said one of the mothers:

'I'm a Cockney born and bred and I sound it and I know it too. Now I know Alice feels it a bit that her parents don't have the same background as the people she mixes with. I've nothing in common with Alice's friends and they've nothing in common with me. I even know it with Janice (a grandchild). I go out to stay with them; Janice says to me, "Are you going to help me, Granny?" I try to follow in her book all these algebra things; she says, "You can understand, can't you?" and I say, "No, I can't," and she says "But it's common sense, and you've got common sense haven't you?" and I say, "Yes, I've got common sense but I can't understand." '

Some of the women feel guilty because they had the chances which their parents and siblings did not have. 'Oh yes, I'm the star in the family, it's awful because they are all bright really. Although my mother's not got the education, she's a thinker.' But whatever the evidence of strain, most of the women passed it over and emphatically denied that their education had made any fundamental difference to their behaviour with their families. They said that the years of sacrifice, when their mothers had stinted themselves for the sake of their schooling, had created a bond which had lasted, and would last. The unity of the family has stood the test of time. So has the tie between mother and daughter, which had to be strong in the first place for grammar school attendance to be possible at all. Whatever their station and whatever their private feelings, our informants all professed loyalty to their family of origin. In this they were no different from their sisters of Bethnal Green.

The main conclusion, in so far as any can be drawn from this small inquiry, is that social ascent achieved by means of school does not raise any more of a barrier within the family than social ascent achieved by other means. Upon the grammar-school pupils, no less than upon the brothers and sisters discussed at the beginning of this chapter, the occupational system wields its influence through geography. People climb into more highly paid jobs and, whether they do it with or without the help of a school teacher, they move away from the lowlands of East London to the more leafy suburbs. When they move, they have less to do with their relatives. Tension – we have caught a hint of it now and then – may arise just because one member of a family is more 'successful' than others. But, in this district, social mobility appears to have no marked independent influence except as it promotes geographical mobility. This chapter does not therefore diminish the importance of change in residence which was borne in upon us by our investigation in Greenleigh.

When visiting the daughters now living in their own homes in the suburbs, we sometimes forgot where we were. The same trim gardens, the same bright parlours, the same neat kitchens – even the same remarks about the neighbours.

Ilford: 'It's not as friendly as Bethnal Green was. We're a bit suburban here. They watch each other, especially with clothes, to keep up with one another. I don't bother myself. I'm satisfied with what I have. I don't try to keep up, but I don't mean by that I wouldn't like a car. Of course I would. It's a pleasure to have a car but I'm not worrying.'

Finchley: 'People round here think because they have a few more pennies they are better than you.'

Southgate: 'Janey is rather lonely here, that's the trouble. We don't see any people around here and I don't like her to go out on her own. You don't know who she'll mix with, do you?'

It might have been Greenleigh all over again, with the same kind of people, for all their education, breathing the purer air and yet worried with the same strange problems which emerged on the estate. 'With change of place,' said Hazlitt,[1] 'we change our ideas; nay, our opinions and feelings.' Migration makes a crucial difference to more than kinship.

1. Hazlitt, W. 'On Going a Journey', p. 79.

12

IN CONCLUSION:
PLANNING AND FAMILY LIFE

IN the previous chapters we have been attempting to describe the facts. Here, in this final chapter, we will no longer strive after impartiality, and, with an eye on future research, relate not so much the facts as some of our own speculations about their meaning. We shall also give some of our own opinions about the housing policy whose effects we have considered.

The view we have formed and tested more or less daily for three years is that very few people wish to leave the East End. They are attached to Mum and Dad, to the markets, to the pubs and settlements, to Club Row and the London Hospital. There are, of course, exceptions. Some people (as mentioned in the previous chapter) have secured a job, or wish for one, in another part of the country, and where job calls, family must usually follow. If there are so few people in Bethnal Green under this necessity to move, it is because the local economy, far from being tied to one industry, offers such a variety of manual work. Social ascent (as it is called) has also been quite rare. The people are manual workers, and, compared to other social classes, these are not nowadays the most on the move.

Some wives also wish to leave because they have fallen out with their own relatives, and more husbands because they cannot get on with their in-laws. When kinship relations go wrong, they can become intolerable. To prevent such people from starting an independent life elsewhere would be even less defensible than to prevail upon the majority to move away from relatives against their will. People should obviously have as much choice of residence as possible: given choice, they will be able to meet best the individual needs of which they, and they only, should be the judge.

We suggest that the majority wish to stay in the East End. If this opinion is to carry any weight, we must try to say why. The first point – one we have made before but will repeat – is that they are tied to the district by time. In some places people divide their lives into two, in one home while they are growing up, and another, far off, when they marry. In Bethnal Green there is no sharp division. People do not, after marriage, throw off the past which contains their former family and friends. They combine past and present. They continue to belong to the same community, and, since the sense of belonging which comes from knowing and being known by so many of their fellow residents is something which most Bethnal Greeners prize, this alone goes some way to explain their attachment.

But their sense of belonging cannot be explained simply by long residence. It is so deep because it is rooted in a lasting attachment to their families. In this, Bethnal Green may be unlike other districts and other classes in which children appear, from superficial observation, to draw away from their parents when they grow up. If this be true – only further research can show – the difference may be related not only to the occupations they follow, but also to the different length of 'childhood'. In the middle classes children are usually dependent on parents until they are adult; their delay in reaching economic independence may make the break all the more complete when at last it does come. On the other hand, in Bethnal Green, as in other working-class districts, nearly all the people left school at fourteen or fifteen and were earning their living not long after puberty, at an age when their fellows in other classes were still sitting at school-desks. Some of them did (and certainly do) use that independence to assert their own personalities by making at least a partial break from their families while still adolescent. Having previously experienced some freedom from parental influence, the women at least seem ready, by the time of marriage, to re-form their ties with their families of origin.

The local kinship system, as we have said again and again,

stresses the tie between mother and daughter; and, if we are to understand the disinclination to move, it is the strength of this tie that we should say a word about, even if we cannot hope to explain it at all fully within the small ambit of this study. The initial group is everywhere parents and children, not just mother and daughters. Sons too are in the cradle. Why then should a closer tie between mother and daughter than between the son and either of his parents crystallize out of the initial situation?

It was probably not always like this. Before Britain was industrialized the bond between father and son was probably no less enduring. After a long apprenticeship on the parental holding, at least one of the sons knew enough of the vagaries of soil and stream, animal and crop, and was, by dint of long indoctrination, attached enough to the family's plot of earth to become devoted to husbandry and to live on in his father's house.[1] Father and son, as well as mother and daughter, were linked not only by family but by their common property rights and by their common occupation, this being also true of the handicraft industries which survived for so long as part of the British economy.[2] In modern times, although the practice has no more entirely disappeared from Bethnal Green than from anywhere else, sons more rarely follow in their father's footsteps. They more often get different jobs, and, when they do, they no longer share the same associations. But the woman's economy has not become so diverse as the man's. Despite the arrival of the doctor and the teacher, child-rearing cannot, by its nature, be subjected to the same division of labour, the same specialization, as the work that men do. Daughters, since they still follow their mothers and inherit the same occupation, continue to have a host of interests in common. These bonds, important still, probably counted even more

1. Some hints are given in some contemporary studies about the persisting importance of the father-son tie in rural areas of the British Isles. See Rees, A. D. *Life in a Welsh Countryside*, p. 72 and Arensberg, C. M. and Kimball, S. T. *Family and Community in Ireland*, p. 80.
2. See Dobb, M. *Studies in the Development of Capitalism*, pp. 262–7.

in the earlier days of factory industry, when the mother-centred kinship system served to give working-class women some security in a life beset by its opposite. The insecurity of men was translated into an even greater lack of security for women, who needed it more, then as always. In a district like Bethnal Green, wives could not rely upon their husbands to stand by them while they reared their children. Death too often removed the prop. Nor were they assured of support from husbands whose lives were spared. In an unstable economy, nearly all men were at some time unemployed and at all times frightened of it; and (as we saw in the opening chapter) even when they were in work, they frequently kept their families short of money. So the wife had to cling to the family into which she was born, and in particular to her mother, as the only other means of ensuring herself against isolation. One or other member of her family would, if need be, relieve her distress, lend her money, or share to some degree in the responsibility for her children. The extended family was her trade union, organized in the main by women and for women, its solidarity her protection against being alone. It is, to judge by anthropology, almost a universal rule that when married life is insecure, the wife turns for support to her family of origin, so that a weak marriage tie produces a strong blood tie.[1] East London does not seem to have been an exception.

Such defensive action might, ironically, produce the very result it was designed to guard against. Aware that the wife's overriding attachment was to her family of origin, excluded from the warmth and intimacy of the female circle, resentful husbands were only too likely to react by withdrawing themselves to their own consolations outside the home, in the pub and in *their* families of origin. The process was a circular one, the husband's withdrawal making her cling to her

1. Some extreme examples of mother-centred extended families are to be found in the West Indies and the Southern States of America, where 'husbands' at one time drifted away as easily as they drifted in. See Henriques, F. M. *Family and Colour in Jamaica*, p. 110, etc., and Frazier, E. F. *The Negro Family in the United States*, p. 125, etc.

mother, and her action making the husband withdraw: insecurity bred insecurity.[1] In Bethnal Green, even today, social workers still lay the blame for some desertions and divorces upon Mum's sometimes far from benign influence. The two-way repercussion of insecurity upon kinship cannot be documented from historical investigation. It is rare to find a mention like Lady Bell's: 'The affectionate relation between the young married daughter and her own home, indeed, sometimes causes an additional difficulty, as there are cases where the young wife neglects her own house to go to her mother's.'[2] But though we cannot document the process, the witness of our informants in Bethnal Green leaves no doubt that, here at any rate, insecurity and kinship were inextricably bound together. The conditions of the past have, we believe, given a certain cast to the kinship system which can still be observed, in some families, to the present day, and whose influence is still felt in the moral code with which that system is surrounded.

*

The daughter's attachment to her mother is no longer such a compelling necessity now that the economy is more stable, broken homes fewer, the birth-rate lower, and the husband's role in the home different. But she still stands to gain a great deal from the person with whom she can share the mysteries as well as the tribulations, the burdens as well as the satisfactions, of child-birth and motherhood. Child-rearing is arduous, it is puzzling, it is monotonous, and the person on whom the primary responsibility falls, if usually on her own when her husband is out at work, may be hard put to avoid the loneliness and exasperation of being confined, day in,

1. Of another place, an anthropologist has written that 'Time and again the instability of Hausa marriage and the high incidence of divorce is seen to be closely linked with the attachment of wives to their kin, an attachment which usually overrides any fondness they may feel for their husbands when they conflict, which frequently happens at the instigation of kinswomen of a senior generation.' Smith, M. G. Intro. to Smith, M. F. *Baba of Karo*, p. 13.

2. Bell, Lady, *At the Works*, p. 169.

day out, in her one-person workplace. She may, if she cannot get any respite, find the five or ten years' hard labour of bringing up her children too exacting and continuous to bear with patience; and if she suffers, so will her children. But with a companion – and who more obvious for her to claim than the woman with whom she has shared her previous life? – her work can be less arduous because it is shared; her life less lonely because she has someone to talk to; the behaviour of her children less perplexing because she has someone whose experience she can draw on; and her lot less monotonous because she can, for the occasional evening or day, leave her children in someone else's care. Whenever the harmony between them exceeds the strife, the wife has something to gain from the help of her mother.

The two women can cooperate so effectively because the younger has not only the same work, but has learnt how to do it from the older woman. Sons, as we have said, usually earn their living at something so different from their fathers that they cannot so often be their pupils as they were in the past. Even when sons follow the same trade, the change in technique from one generation to another may be so great that they have, in their apprenticeship, to attend to other masters. Not that the women's world is static. Techniques of housekeeping and fashions in child-care also change, and the faster the rate, the quicker the obsolescence of the mother's skill. The improvement in the technical equipment of the home may yet change the mother-daughter relationship, for instance, by making the daughter her mother's teacher as well as pupil, as much as the improvement in the technical equipment of the farm has, we are told, weakened the authority of the farmer over his son.[1] But changes in the home are less revolutionary, and easier to assimilate, than changes in industry. Technical progress has removed only part of education from the home; long after either she or her husband has ceased to be one for their son, the mother

[1] See Williams, W. M. *The Sociology of an English Village: Gosforth*, p. 44.

191

is for her daughter a teacher who accustoms her to a particular way of doing things in the home, and the daughter,
since her ways are also her mother's, is likely to feel that
she can trust the good sense of her helper.

The benefit is not all one-sided. For the grandmothers
and grandfathers the gain is even more obvious. They too,
as old age draws on, are even more likely to be lonely than
their daughters, and oppressed by their uselessness. If they
have children and grandchildren around them, they can
not only be of some value to youth, they can also enjoy
the reward of being appreciated; and, as they watch over
their grandchildren, they can perhaps find some comfort
in this evidence of the continuity of life. In their declining
years they can call on their descendants to complete the
circle of care by easing the strain of infirmity, illness, and
bereavement. In a three-generation family the old as well
as the young both receive and give services; the aid is
reciprocal.[1]

We are certainly not suggesting that the family can be
self-sufficient. Although three generations can muster more
resources than two, there are still many essential services
which no family can possibly provide for itself. Few grandmothers can perform operations or teach algebra. Few
grandfathers can, on their own, maintain children stricken
by illness or unemployment. Children, unaided, cannot
support their parents through the years of retirement. The
family is not a society on its own, merely part of the wider
society, and, if it is to perform its proper function w:thin its
own sphere, the family needs the support which only the
wider society can give. This vital support the social services
in some measure already supply. The health services have
made a great and obvious difference to the well-being of the
family, especially to mothers and children. Old age pen-
sions, inadequate though they often are, have enabled
children to care for their parents all the more effectively.
Anthropologists have reported how much even the old

1. The meaning of kinship for the old is explored in Townsend, P.
The Family Life of Old People.

non-contributory pension sweetened relations between the generations in Ireland,[1] and what is true there is just as much true in East London. The social services have in many ways already made the family of three generations or two not less, but more, viable, and perhaps the administrators will be in a position to do even more as knowledge accumulates of the structure and needs of family life.

Nor are we suggesting that the three-generation family has advantages for all women, let alone for all men. Some people favour the extended family, others the isolated household. It all depends on the individual. We do not know which kind of personality, in woman or man, old or young, flourishes in the one rather than the other. Personality, far from being an independent variable, is probably related to family structure. But we can at present hardly even guess which kind of family produces which kind of person. In what way, if at all, are children reared by one mother on her own different from children reared by mothers intimately assisted by grandmothers?[2] This is the kind of question which psychology should in time be able to illuminate, and thus add another, and vital, dimension to our understanding of kinship. For the moment, all we can say for certain is that, for one reason or another, whether rightly or wrongly, most of the women we have interviewed think they get advantages from their attachment to their mothers.

Though they both derive benefit from the relationship, it is far more than a mere arrangement for mutual convenience. The attachment between them is supported by a powerful moral code. This moral code which surrounds kinship is sometimes harsh, imprisoning the human spirit and stunting growth and self-expression, and sometimes observed only in its outward forms. But it need not be so. In most of these families (and Bethnal Green is obviously unexceptional in this) duty and affection seem to coexist and, indeed, reinforce

1. Arensberg, C. M. and Kimball, S. T. op. cit., pp. 125–6.
2. One kind of effect upon personality of being brought up in a wider circle of kin has been noted by Mead, M. in *Coming of Age in Samoa,* pp. 168–9.

each other, duty fostering affection as much as affection fosters duty. Parents do not choose their children, nor children their parents; the relationship exists whether or not either has the qualities which might arouse affection. Both are usually accepted despite their faults, the dutiful parent not discarding the child born mentally defective nor the dutiful child the parent who has committed what is a crime in the eyes of the greater world; and what applies to parents and children applies in some measure to other relatives as well. Secure in the knowledge that they are valued because they are members of the family, not because they have this or that quality or achievement to their credit, they respond with affection which then becomes as reciprocal as duty. Affection, for its part, helps to make duty not so much the nicely balanced correlative of rights as a more or less unlimited liability beyond the bounds of self-interest and rational calculation. The mother does not inquire whether she will be repaid before she does the washing for her sick daughter, the daughter whether she can afford the time to nurse her mother through a long illness.

*

Though we have taken our cue from East London, our remarks on the three-generation family are expressed in general terms. If what we say is correct, then we would expect to find the same kind of system, the same stressing of the mother-daughter tie, in other places, and especially in other working-class districts. For the few other places where previous investigations have been made, there is in fact some evidence of this kind. Miss Shaw could as well have been writing of Bethnal Green when she reported on working-class families in Acton.

The grandmothers, especially the maternal grandmother, played an important part in the lives of many of the families. Nearly one-third of the seventy families who had children living at home either had grannies, or *were* grannies, living locally and in close contact. They were the child-minders for their married daughters who went out to work; they were called in to help in confinements or illnesses; and they were consulted on the upbringing of the children. It was to the grandmother's home that the scattered family returned for the major social events – weddings, christenings, engagement parties, and Christmas and birthday parties.[1]

Dr Kerr has written in rather the same terms of some streets in a working-class quarter of Liverpool.

Both Jamaica and Ship Street are flourishing matriarchies. In both a certain amount of lip service is paid to the male, but the chief female in the family is the pivot and the boss . . . Because of this very complete reliance on the Mum the children find it very difficult or indeed impossible to leave home. In Ship Street the majority of women after marriage live either with their Mum, or as near as possible in the same street or just in the next street.[2]

Professor Firth and Judith Djamour have also described a not dissimilar family structure in 'South Borough', a London borough only a few miles 'over the water' from Bethnal Green.

The question of kinship grouping has especial reference to the critical role of wife/mother in the system. It is clear that this woman is a key figure in South Borough kinship. In terms of emotional relationship, communication, and services . . . the tie between a mother and her children is normally very strong, and tends to remain so throughout her life. Mother and married daughter are commonly in frequent, often daily, contact, and a married son also tends to visit his mother at least weekly, if possible. Continuity between households forming a kinship network is usually provided largely by the mother. This is epitomized by the remark of one informant that 'in England, at Christmas, all the children and in-laws go to Mother's', and by that of another,' Since my mother died, we've all drifted away.' We might speak then of South Borough kinship as being *matri-centred* or *matral* in action, and in sentiment.[3]

These investigations are, like Dr Sheldon's inquiry in Wolverhampton, as much local as our own. Yet if our argument

1. Shaw, L. A. 'Impressions of Family Life in a London Suburb', p. 183.
2. Kerr, M. *Comparative Study of Deprivation in Jamaica and Liverpool.* See also Kerr, M. *The People of Ship Street*, Chapters IV and XVI.
3. Firth, R. and Djamour, J. 'Kinship in South Borough', p. 41.

is right, we would expect the stressing of the mother-daughter tie to be a widespread, perhaps universal, phenomenon in the urban areas of all industrial countries, at any rate in the families of manual workers. Future research will show whether this expectation is justified.

*

In this chapter we set out to say why most people are attached to the district, and this has led us to consider some of the advantages, for wives in particular, of the local kinship system. The reason they do not want to leave the borough is that its effectiveness depends a good deal upon the geographical proximity of the key figures. During the stages of their lives when they are most in need of support, neither wives nor their mothers can easily move about. If they have babies and young children to look after, the wives cannot readily make longer journeys than they can easily navigate with a pram. Nor can aged parents easily travel far. The mobility of both is often small. This is all the more severe a limitation if they have little money to pay for transport, and little of the time-sense and organizing power which enable some people to maintain a kind of cohesion in a widely scattered circle of friends and relatives. Migration by young couples interposes a barrier of distance which impedes the reciprocal flow of services between the generations. Hence the significance of the move of only a few miles to Greenleigh.

It seems that when the balance of a three-generation family is disturbed, the task of caring for dependants at both ends of life, always one of the great and indispensable functions of any society, becomes less manageable. Dr Sheldon has underlined the consequences for the old of such a disturbance.

'The enormous building developments in this country since the war have,' he says, 'been devoted in the main to the needs of the immediate family of parents and children and are not necessarily so well suited to the care of three generations. One way in which many families used to cope with this problem has unintentionally been made more difficult by the shift, mainly of the younger generation, out to the new dwellings. Both the old people and their younger relatives are agreed on the layout most suitable for many families which can be summed up as one of independent propinquity – i.e., separate establishments sited reasonably close to each other, so combining the advantages of independence and ready mutual aid. The movement away of the younger generation inevitably leaves more old people who can no longer depend on the ready accessibility of their children; but it is essential to recognize this aspect of the natural history of old age and to assist a desire of the two generations to live closer to each other, for otherwise we are depriving ourselves of what has hitherto been one of the principal methods by which so many families have elected to care for their old people.'[1]

In a three-generation family the burden of caring for the young as well, though bound to fall primarily on the mothers, can be lightened by being shared with the grandmothers. The three generations complement each other. Once prise out two of them, and the wives are left without the help of grandmothers, the old without the comfort of children and grandchildren.

＊

The question for the authorities is whether they should do more than they are at present doing to meet the preference of people who would not willingly forgo these advantages, rather than insisting that more thousands should migrate beyond the city. To supply good houses for families with young children as well as flats for others is not a simple operation in a congested town; we do not pretend that it is. It would mean sacrificing some of the many projected open spaces, earmarked in the plans for future public gardens and parks, for the only reason which could justify so grave a step, that on balance people would much rather have houses than spaces. It would mean putting some factories rather than residences in high flatted buildings. It might mean gradually

1. Sheldon, J. H. 'The Social Philosophy of Old Age', Presidential Address to the Third Congress of the International Association of Gerontology, p. 25.

moving out to the country some of the vast railway yards, the unwelcome inheritance of another transport age, which at present sprawl smokily across the face of the city – and using the sites for houses instead. It would certainly mean saving as many as possible of the existing houses, where these are structurally sound, by installing within the old fabric new bathrooms, lavatories, and kitchens. The problems are formidable, but if the purpose of rehousing is to meet human needs, not as they are judged by others but as people themselves assess their own, it is doubtful whether anything short of such a programme will suffice.

Not everyone could, under this or any other plan, hope to stay where he is. People will have to move about within their own district, if not outside it, as the slums beyond salvage are cleared and replaced. But re-shuffling the residents could be accomplished by moving as a block the social groups, above all the wider families, to which people wish to belong. Movement of street and kinship groupings as a whole, members being transferred together to a new setting, would enable the city to be rebuilt without squandering the fruits of social cohesion.

The physical size of reconstruction is so great that the authorities have been understandably intent upon bricks and mortar. Their negative task is to demolish slums which fall below the most elementary standards of hygiene, their positive one to build new houses and new towns cleaner and more spacious than the old. Yet even when the town planners have set themselves to create communities anew as well as houses, they have still put their faith in buildings, sometimes speaking as though all that was necessary for neighbourliness was a neighbourhood unit, for community spirit a community centre. If this were so, then there would be no harm in shifting people about the country, for what is lost could soon be regained by skilful architecture and design. But there is surely more to a community than that. The sense of loyalty to each other amongst the inhabitants of a place like Bethnal Green is not due to buildings. It is due far more to ties of kinship and friendship which connect the *people* of one household to the *people* of another. In such a district community spirit does not have to be fostered, it is already there. If the authorities regard that spirit as a social asset worth preserving, they will not uproot more people, but build the new houses around the social groups to which they already belong.

LIST OF REFERENCES

Arensberg, C. M. and Kimball, S. T., *Family and Community in Ireland*. Cambridge, Mass., Harvard University Press, 1948.

Bakke, E. W., *The Unemployed Man*. London, Nisbet, 1933.

Bell, Lady, *At the Works*. London, Edward Arnold, 1907.

Booth, C., *Life and Labour of the People in London*. 17 vols. London, Macmillan, 1902.

Bosanquet, Helen, *Rich and Poor*. London, Macmillan, 1899.
　　The Family. London, Macmillan, 1906.

Bourdillon, A. F. C. (ed.), *Voluntary Social Services*, London, Methuen, 1945.

Bowley, A. L. and Burnett-Hurst, A. R., *Livelihood and Poverty*. London, Bell, 1915.

Cornwell, J., *Hard-Earned Lives*. London, Tavistock, 1984.

Dennis, N., Henriques, F., and Slaughter, C., *Coal is Our Life*. London, Eyre & Spottiswoode, 1956.

Dobb, M., *Studies in the Development of Capitalism*. London, Kegan Paul, 1946.

Dunleavey, P., *The Politics of Mass Housing in Britain 1945–1975*. Oxford, Clarendon Press, 1981.

Durant, R., *Watling: A Survey of Social Life on a New Housing Estate*. London, P. S. King, 1939.

Firth, R. (ed.), *Two Studies of Kinship in London*. London School of Economics, Monographs on Social Anthropology, No. 15. University of London, The Athlone Press, 1956.

Firth, R. and Djamour, J., 'Kinship in South Borough'. See Firth, R. (ed.), *Two Studies of Kinship in London*.

Frazier, E. F., *The Negro Family in the United States*. Chicago, University of Chicago Press, 1939.

Glass, D. V. (ed.), *Social Mobility in Britain*. London, Routledge & Kegan Paul, 1954.

Glass, R. and Frenkel, M., 'How they Live at Bethnal Green'. *Contact: Britain Between West and East*. London, Contact Publications Limited, 1946.

Gorer, G., *Exploring English Character*. London, The Cresset Press, 1955.

LIST OF REFERENCES

Hall, J. and Jones, D. C., 'Social Grading of Occupations'. *British Journal of Sociology*, Vol. 1, No. 1, March 1950.

Hall, P., Thomas, R., Gracey, H. and Drewett, R., *The Containment of Urban England*, two volumes. London, George Allen and Unwin, 1973.

Hazlitt, W., 'On Going a Journey'. *Selected Essays*. Ed. Keynes, G., London, The Nonesuch Press, 1930.

Henriques, F. M., *Family and Colour in Jamaica*. London, Eyre & Spottiswoode, 1953.

Himmelweit, H. T., 'Social Status and Secondary Education since the 1944 Act: Some Data for London'. See Glass, D. V. (ed.), *Social Mobility in Britain*.

Holme, A., *Housing and Young Families in East London*. London, Routledge and Kegan Paul, 1985.

Inner London Education Authority, *Educational Priority Index: Changes Between 1983 and 1985*. ILEA 5130, 1985.

Kerr, M., *Comparative Study of Deprivation in Jamaica and Liverpool*. Paper delivered to British Association, 1953. Much of this paper was repeated in Kerr, M., 'The Study of Personality Deprivation through Projection Tests', *Social and Economic Studies* (University College of the West Indies), Vol. 4, No. 1, March 1955.

    The People of Ship Street. London, Routledge and Kegan Paul, 1958.

Matthews, W., *Cockney Past and Present*. London, George Routledge & Sons, 1938.

Mayhew, H., *London Labour and the London Poor*. 2 vols. London, George Woodfall & Son, 1851.

Mead, M., *Coming of Age in Samoa*. London, Penguin Books, 1954.

Mitchell, G. D. and Lupton, T., 'The Liverpool Estate'. See *Neighbourhood and Community*.

Mumford, L., *City Development*. London, Secker & Warburg, 1946.

Munby, D. L., *Industry and Planning in Stepney*. London, Oxford University Press, 1951.

Parsons, T., 'The Kinship System of the Contemporary United States'. *Essays in Sociological Theory Pure and Applied*. Glencoe, Illinois, The Free Press, 1949.

Potter, B., 'The Jewish Community'. See Booth, C., *Life and Labour of the People in London*, Vol. 3.

Radcliffe-Brown, A. R., 'On Joking Relationships'. *Structure and Function in Primitive Society: Essays and Addresses*. London, Cohen & West, 1952.

Radcliffe-Brown, A. R. and Forde, D. (ed.), *African Systems of Kinship and Marriage.* London, Oxford University Press, 1950.

Rees, A. D., *Life in a Welsh Countryside.* Cardiff, University of Wales Press, 1951.

Reeves, M. S., *Round about a Pound a Week.* London, Bell, 1913.

Robb, J. H., *Working-Class Anti-Semite.* London, Tavistock Publications, 1954.

Rose, M., *The East End of London.* London; The Cresset Press, 1951.

Rowntree, B. S., *Poverty and Progress.* London, Longmans, 1941.

Self, P. J. O., 'Voluntary Organisations in Bethnal Green'. See Bourdillon, A. F. C. (ed.), *Voluntary Social Services.*

Shankland, G., Willmott, P. and Jordan, D., *Inner London: Policies for Dispersal and Balance.* London: Her Majesty's Stationery Office, 1977.

Shaw, L. A., 'Impressions of Family Life in a London Suburb'. *The Sociological Review*, New Series, Vol. 2, No. 2, December 1954.

Sheldon, J. H., *The Social Medicine of Old Age.* London, Oxford University Press, 1948.

'The Social Philosophy of Old Age'. Presidential Address to the Third Congress of the International Association of Gerontology. *Old Age in the Modern World.* London, Livingstone, 1955.

Sinclair, R., *East London.* London, Robert Hale, 1950.

Slater, E. and Woodside, M., *Patterns of Marriage.* London, Cassell, 1951.

Smith, M. F., *Baba of Karo: A Woman of the Muslim Hausa.* London, Faber and Faber, 1954.

Titmuss, R. M., *Problems of Social Policy.* London, H.M.S.O. and Longmans, 1950.

'The Position of Women'. *Essays on the Welfare State.* London, Allen & Unwin, 1958.

Townsend, P., *The Family Life of Old People.* London, Routledge & Kegan Paul, 1957.

Williams, W. M., *The Sociology of an English Village: Gosforth.* London, Routledge & Kegan Paul, 1956.

Willmott, P., *The Evolution of a Community.* London, Routledge and Kegan Paul, 1963.

Young, M., 'Distribution of Income within the Family'. *British Journal of Sociology*, Vol. III, No. 4, December 1952.

'The Role of the Extended Family in a Disaster'. *Human Relations*, Vol. VII, No. 3, 1954.

LIST OF REFERENCES

Young, M. and Willmott, P., 'Social Grading by Manual Workers'. *British Journal of Sociology*, Vol. VII, No. 4, December 1956.

Young, M., Young, H., Shuttleworth, E. and Tucker, W., *Report from Hackney*. London, Policy Studies Institute, 1981.

Young, T., *Becontree and Dagenham*. London, Becontree Social Survey Committee, 1934.

Census, 1951. Great Britain. 1 per cent Sample Tables. London, H.M.S.O., 1952.
　　England and Wales. County Report, London. London, H.M.S.O., 1953.
　　England and Wales. Occupation Tables. London, H.M.S.O., 1956.
　　England and Wales. Report on Usual Residence and Workplace. London, H.M.S.O., 1956.

Classification of Occupations, 1950. London, H.M.S.O., 1951.

The Dock Worker. The University of Liverpool, Department of Social Science. The University Press of Liverpool, 1954.

Early Leaving. A Report of the Central Advisory Council for Education (England). Ministry of Education, London, H.M.S.O., 1954.

London Housing Statistics, 1954–55, London County Council, October 1955.

Maternity in Great Britain. Joint Committee of the Royal College of Obstetricians and Gynaecologists and the Population Investigation Committee. London, Oxford University Press, 1948.

Neighbourhood and Community. Social Research Series. The University Press of Liverpool, 1954.

The Paperworker. Journal of the National Union of Printing, Bookbinding, and Paper Workers.

Review of the Work of the National Dock Labour Board 1947–9. London, National Dock Labour Board, March 1950.

INDEX

INDEX

Council employment, 96–7
Courting, 70–71

Dagenham estate, 123, 129n., 167–8
Death-rate, falling, 21–2
Density of population, 153, 197–8
Dock work, 97–100
Durant, R., 129n., 150n.
Dwellings, sharing of, 23, 31–3, 34–5, 38, 66
See also Housing, sharing of

Earnings,
 low in past, 17
 maximum when young, 94
 of husbands not known to wives, 18, 26–7
Education,
 grammar-school, and social mobility, 174–85
 in home, 191
 public money spent on, 146
 secondary, attitude to, 28–30, 162n.
 uniformity of, at Bethnal Green, 94
Evacuation, 123–4, 128–9
Extended family,
 absent at Greenleigh, 132–3
 combination of families of origin and marriage, 48
 daughter member of mother's, 60–61
 husband drawn into wife's, 68–70, 71–2, 73
 mother's sister member of, 82–3
 siblings members of, 78, 87–8
 women's trade union, 189

Families, broken. *See* Broken homes
Family,
 definitions of, 12–13, 48
 extended. *See* Extended family
 two- and three-generation, 192–7

Family clubs, 45, 80, 136, 140
Family of marriage,
 definition, 12
 status at Greenleigh, 163
 See also Marriage
Family of origin,
 definition of, 12
 parent's, 83–6
Family size. *See* Birth-rate
Fathers,
 as grandfathers, 58–60
 frequency of contact with, 45–6
 inheritance of Christian names by sons, 25–6
 link with sons in past, 188
 succession in jobs by sons, 97–102
Fertility, 20–21
Firth, R., 195
Flats, 127, 197
Flowers,
 and war memorials, 110
 love of, by Huguenots, 114
French descent, 113–14
Frequency of contact with relatives,
 and social class, 171–4, 181–2
 at Greenleigh, 131–8
 with parents, 45–6, 48–9, 67–8, 126, 182
 with siblings, 77, 83
 with uncles and aunts, 83
Friends,
 in Bethnal Green, 104–18, 132
 at Greenleigh, 147–64
 loss of, for grammar-school children in past, 176
 through school, 61
 through work, 61, 63

Garages, 159
Gardens,
 as symbols of status, 155
 at Greenleigh, 121, 132, 145–6
 in middle-class districts, 184
 influence on standards of living, 157

206

See also Mother, Mothers and daughters

Mothers and daughters,
conflicts with husbands, 64–8
contacts between, 45–6, 137
day-to-day relations between, 46–7, 55–6
exchange of services, 50–56
influence of grammar-school education on, 184
tie stressed in other areas, 194–6
why close tie between, 187–94
See also Mother, Mothers

Mumford, L., 111

Names of children and parents, 25–6
Names of informants, fictitious, 13
National Dock Labour Board, 98–100
Neighbours,
in Bethnal Green, 104–18, 132
in Greenleigh, 142, 147–64

Occupations. *See* Class, social; Bethnal Green, industries
Old People, The Family Life of, 56n., 192n.
Overcrowding, 23–4, 127

Parents,
frequency of contact with, 45–6, 48–9, 67–8, 126, 182
preference for living near, 35
residence of, 31–7
Parsons, T., 170
Patrilocal residence, 37
Population Investigation Committee, 150
Poverty,
and social research, 17–18
before the last war, 28
Public houses, 109
difference between Bethnal Green and Greenleigh, 121, 142, 145, 153
in the past, 23–4

Radcliffe-Brown, A. R., 58n., 67n., 69n.
Reeves, M. S., 18n.
Refusals,
general sample, 13
Rehousing, 123–4, 168–9
Relatives,
help in getting houses, 41–2
help in getting job, 94–7
living at Greenleigh, 125, 131
residence of. *See* Residence of relatives
See also Fathers, Frequency of contact with relatives, Mothers, Mothers and daughters, Parents, Siblings, Uncles and aunts
Rents, 135, 143–4
Residence, continuity of. *See* Continuity of residence
Residence of relatives
and frequency of contact, 49, 172, 182
at Greenleigh, 125, 131
distance from Greenleigh, 158–9
effects on kinship, 114–18, 150–53, 165
ex-grammar-school girls, 181–3
in Bethnal Green, 86–7
in precinct, 110
in same street, 108–9
parents, 31–7
Ritual occasions, 84–6, 138, 195
Robb, J. H., 110
Rowntree, 19, 27

Sample,
general, 13
grammar school, 174
Greenleigh, 122
Samples,
description of, 13
marriage, 13
Schools,
further away at Greenleigh, 144

INDEX

Schools—*cont.*
  grammar, and social mobility,
    174–85
  public money spent on, 146
  pressure on, at Greenleigh, 167
  private boarding, 182
  secondary, choice of, 29, 162n.
Sheldon, J. H., 36, 43, 48, 195,
  196–7
Shops, 109, 121, 142, 144, 153
Siblings,
  as godparents, 84–5
  at christenings, 84–5
  contacts and social class of,
    171–4
  eldest as head of family, 79–81,
    85
  influence of mother on relations
    with, 76–8
  kept together by mother's
    memory, 78–9
  parents', 83–4
  unmarried, 81–2
Significance, statistical,
  of grammar school inquiry, 175
Single people,
  attachments to siblings, 82
  residence of, 81–2
Slums, 41–2, 110, 198
Social change,
  caused by housing estates, 124
  in Bethnal Green, 17–30
  in the home, 191–2
Social grading inquiry, 29n.
Street parties, 109

Telephones, 157–9
Television,
  as means of education, 183
  as symbol of status, 156n.

examples, 27, 59, 132
high cost of, 143
need for at Greenleigh, 143, 149
Tenancy, 33–4, 39–42, 66
Tenement buildings, 38, 40–41, 44
Titmuss, R. M., 22, 28
Trade unions, 94–103
Travel to work, 91–2, 93, 133,
  135, 144, 158
'Turnings', 109

Uncles and aunts, 83–8
  frequency of contact with, 83

Victoria Park, 116
Visiting, 107–8, 132, 136–7, 142

Wages, 94, 139
  See also Earnings
War memorials, 109–10
Watling estate, 129n., 150n.
Weddings, 62–4, 85–6
Welfare service, 53, 56, 192
Work, married women's, 21, 54–5,
  133, 149
Working class, 171–85
  at Greenleigh, 122, 159
  children compared to middle
    class, 187
  defined by occupation, 13
  distribution of, in Bethnal
    Green, 93
  families in other districts, 194–6
  husbands in, 17–19, 27, 30
  judgements of status, 29
  migration of, 11
  property-rights in, 33–4
  wives at childbirth, 50
  See also Class, social
Working hours, 24